MW00335360

Motion Offense:
The Principles of the
Five-Man Open Post

Bob Huggins

©2008 Coaches Choice. All rights reserved. Printed in the United States.

No part of this book may be reproduced, stored in a retrieval system, or transmitted, in any form or by any means, electronic, mechanical, photocopying, recording, or otherwise, without the prior permission of Coaches Choice.

ISBN: 978-1-58518-333-3
Library of Congress Catalog Card Number: 00-107306
Cover design: Jeanne Hamilton and Bean Creek Studio
Front cover photo: Albert Dickson/TSN/Zuma Press©2006 by TSN
Developmental editor: Burrall Paye
Layout design: Jeanne Hamilton

Coaches Choice
P.O. Box 1828
Monterey, CA 93942
www.coacheschoice.com

Contents

Introduction 4

Diagram Key 5

Chapter

1   Basic Movements 7

2   Offense Before Cuts Begin 17

3   Cut-to-the-Basket Options 22

4   Cut-to-the-Ball Options 32

5   Cut-Away-from-the-Ball Options 41

6   Offense from the Wings 45

7   Getting the Corners More Involved 48

8   Weakside Involvement 53

9   Individual & Two-on-Two Drills 58

10   Three-on-Three Drills 69

11   Weakside and Other Drills 76

12   Five Player Open Post as a Multiple Offense 83

13   Team Drilling of the Offensive Strategies
     for the Five Player Open Post Offense 88

     About the Author 92

Introduction

This book was written to provide the reader with an overview of the motion offense we use at the University of Cincinnati. In Chapter 1, the basic movements of the Five Player Open Post Motion Offense are discussed. The basic motion is shown from five perspectives: (1) offense before cuts begin (Chapter 2); (2) cut-to-the-basket options (Chapter 3); (3) cut-to-the-ball options (Chapter 4); (4) cut-away-from-the-ball options (Chapter 5); and (5) offense from the wings (Chapter 6). Each of these five basic patterns is examined in detail in a separate chapter. Everything a coach needs to incorporate this offense into his offensive system receives extensive treatment.

The involvement of corners in the motion offense is presented in Chapter 7. Weakside play, so important in motion offenses, is discussed in Chapter 8. Paramount to properly teaching any offense is intelligent drilling. Chapter 9 offers both individual and two-on-two drills; and Chapter 10 features three-on-three drills. These drills can be used to develop better execution of the offense. The drills can be employed to acheive several objectives, including improving shooting, perfecting the decision-making skills of the players, etc. Weakside drills are included in Chapter 11.

Although this offensive scheme is primarily a person-to-person offense, it can be used with slight adjustments as a multiple offense. With proper variations, the motion offense can be utilized against a myriad of defenses, e.g., zones, combinations, half court traps, and the match-up. This offense can even be operated as a delay, a stall, or to get the last shot of each quarter. Chapter 12 discusses how to make the Five Player Open Post a multiple offense.

As a coach, have you thought about going to a particular player only, or maybe even just two players? You can accomplish that strategy with this offense. Have you given any consideration to requiring your team to shoot only lay ups? Or how about prescribing only short jumpers against sagging defenses? And even designating who you will allow to take those jumpers? With the Five Player Open Post Motion Offense, you can have a mismatch at any position and take advantage of that size or talent differential constantly and repeatedly without even taking a time out. Chapter 13 reviews how to organize your team's practices so that these strategies can be developed.

This offense is simple to teach, easy to learn, and coherent to execute. I hope that your team has as much success with it as we have.

— B.H.

Diagram Key

Every player on a team can begin at any of the positions. Classically, the 1 position is the point guard; the 2 spot is occupied by the shooting guard; the 3 slot is engaged by the shooting forward; the 4 role is performed by the power forward; and the 5 hole is the post person. Initially, each diagram is drawn in this way. Because this offense is a five player open post, all five positions can be functionally filled by five small guards, five big people, or whatever combination best suits a team's personnel.

Flexibility is a major asset of this particular motion offense. Not only can a team play with five big players, or five small guards, or any combination in between, it can actually start its offense with the post man at the 1 position and the point guard at the 2, 3, 4, or 5. This type of changeable option is available to a coach for whatever objective he seeks to accomplish.

If a coach wants to post up his 2 player, for example, he could begin with each player in his classical position and run the cut-to-the-ball option, hand the ball off to 1, and allow the 2 player to cut off 4's screen to proper post position. On the other hand, he could use the dribble entry and let 2 cut directly to the big block.

Defenders will not always be shown in the diagrams. This way of diagramming offers less clutter in the diagram, making them smoother to read, and easier to understand. The point to remember is that throughout the book, X1 guards 1, X2 defends 2, X3 covers 3, X4 checks 4, and X5 blankets 5, even if they do not appear in the diagrams.

After a team runs its fast break into its secondary offense, that team is in proper position, regardless of where the specific players are, to begin this motion offense. The player with the ball merely passes it and either cuts to the basket, cuts to the ball, or cuts away from the ball. Whichever option is chosen activates the next phase of the Five Player Open Post Offense. Throughout the book, not only are the principles of play shown, but also the shot options available from each cut, each movement, and each defensive play.

The following diagram illustrates the KEY to each diagram. Every diagram in this book has 1 at the point, 2 and 3 at the wings, and 4 and 5 in the corners. A team, however, can begin any of its personnel at any of the spots.

All diagrams depict the offense beginning on the left side of the court, making the left side the strongside. The weakside is the right side. This procedure does not mean that the offense is limited to entries to the left side only. When a coach adopts this offense as his own, he can teach it to the right side as well. Entry to the left side is done only to help the reader better understand the smooth flow of the offense.

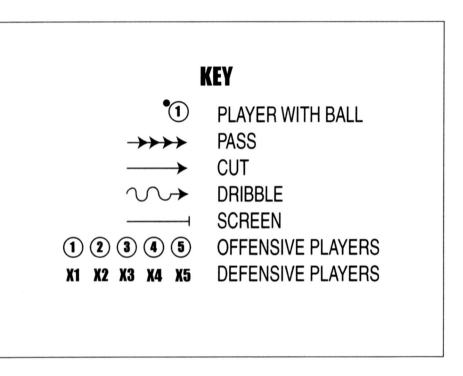

1

Basic Movements

Three major cutting categories exist: (1) cut to the basket, (2) cut to the ball, and (3) cut away from the ball. All three will be covered extensively in this chapter. Two additional aspects also need to be addressed: (1) offense before play begins, and (2) offense from the wings after play has started. Both topics have chapters devoted entirely to them.

Basic Open Post Alignment

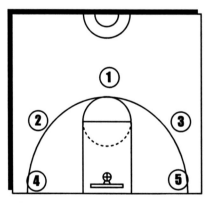

Diagram 1-1

The Five Player Open Post starts from a spread 1-2-2 formation (Diagram 1-1). 1 wants to locate in the middle of the court, a few feet above the key. 2 and 3 are the wing players, and they locate on the free-throw line extended. They want to be a yard or two from the sidelines. 4 and 5 place themselves in the two opposite corners, a yard or two from both the sideline and the baseline.

Rules To Replace

These five positions are kept filled as best as the players can. This objective is accomplished by the following Rule to Replace. It states: *Anytime a player above you begins to cut, you cut immediately to replace*. Let's say 1 begins a cut, and 2 has the ball. Then, it would be 3's job to replace 1 with a cut shown in Diagram 1-2.

3 should cut directly along the line to the ball (2 in Diagram 1-2), parallel to the baseline. This path takes 3 along the free throw line. Why this cut? Because 3 can only be played one of two ways. 3 can be denied the ball. This signals 3 to step outside one step with his right foot, push off hard, and back door his defender, X3. On the other hand, X3 could be sagging on 3. In this case, 3 pushes off his left foot, and replaces 1 at the point. These maneuvers will receive full treatment in Chapter 9 as a two-on-two player drill.

This maneuver by 3 has a two-fold purpose. It keeps his defender out of the play between 2 and the cutting 1. It also gives the offense another cutting option should X3, 3's defender, misplay 3's initial cut. 5 then fills 3's vacated spot, according to the Rule to Replace stated previously.

The second part to the Rules to Replace is: *On any two-person or three-person plays, you replace the opening space*. Diagram 1-3 shows 1 passing to 2 and going to screen for 2. 2 and 1 operate the screen and roll. This is a two-on-two person play. Hence, the corner, 4 in Diagram 1-3, replaces the opening space. This action will be

Diagram 1-2

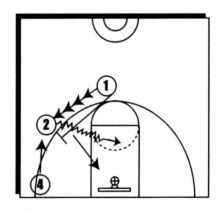

Diagram 1-3

discussed in Chapters 9 and 10 that cover the two-on-two and three-on-three drills respectively. At this point, it is sufficient to demonstrate how the spaces are kept filled per Rules to Replace.

Diagram 1-4 illustrates a three-on-three person play. To follow the Rule to Replace discussed on the previous page, 4 would fill the spot vacated by 1 and 2's actions.

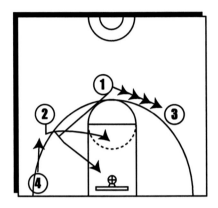

Diagram 1-4

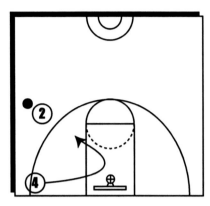

Diagram 1-5

On the strongside area of the court where the ball is, the corner player may cut at any time into the side- or high-post region (Diagram 1-5). Times will exist when the strong-side corner wants to cut to the side- or high-post strongside to clear that side of the court for a two on two play. The strongside corner might also want to get involved in the two-on-two or three-on-three plays by becoming a screener or a pass receiver. Those options are covered in Chapters 9 and 10 when two-on-two and three-on-three plays are discussed. When the strongside corner cuts to the side- or high-post, the corner spot is left vacated. The Rules to Replace permits *any nearby cutter to fill that corner space.*

Back-door cutting on the weakside (i.e., the side of the court away from the basketball) is emphasized in our offense. We want the weakside players to constantly watch their defenders for the opportunity to make this cut. The directive which tells the weakside player when to make the back door cut is covered in Chapter 9.

In Diagram 1-6, 2 thinks he has his defender defeated with a back-door cut. Upon seeing 2 cut to the basket, 4 fills 2's vacated spot. The last Rule to Replace states, *on all weakside back-door or middle cuts, the lower player replaces in the above spot. In addition, all players have the right to always replace themselves with a V cut* (an action that is addressed in Chapter 9) *at any time.*

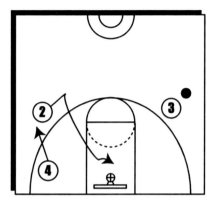

Diagram 1-6

The aforementioned actions have a three-fold purpose:

- They provide constant and immediate movement. As a result, the defender covering the player making the move could make a mistake, thereby creating another opportunity for a cut.

- The V cut is designed to keep the defender on the cutter moving. If he doesn't move with the V cutter, he will allow a back-door or a middle cut to develop for the V cutter. The movement by the defender on the V cutter also keeps that defender out of the play being run by the V cutter's teammates.

- The V cut helps to keep the offensive alignment in a 1-2-2 open post. As a result, the offensive player responsible for defense will be in a defensive position should the ball be turned over or should the defenders get a defensive rebound. It also permits the replacers who are moving to get a head start to the offensive boards. All factors considered, a moving player is much harder to block off the offensive boards.

Rebounding Assignments

We have found either of two methods to be highly successful for keeping balance—i.e., three-and-one-half players to the offensive boards and one-and-one-half players back on defense.

- *Method Number One*: The point guard is assigned to always be back at the half-court area when a shot is taken. Under this system, 2 would go to the free-throw line area as a half defender, half rebounder. 3, 4, and 5 would go hard to the boards.

- *Method Number Two*: The players, who end up in spots 3, 4, and 5 when the shot is taken, storm the offensive boards. The player in the 1 slot goes back to defend at the half-court line. Finally, the player in 2's hole goes to the free-throw area as half rebounder, half defender.

The sole exception to both methods concerns the driving lay-up. Should 1 drive for the lay-up, 2 goes all the way back to half court, and 3 fills the free-throw line extended. Should 2 drive for the lay-up, 1 goes back to the half court line, and 3 goes to the free-throw line extended. All other responsibilities remain the same.

Cuts to the Basket

Cuts to the basket is one of the three major cutting maneuvers. 1 has the first opportunity to cut because he has the ball and must make one of the following three cuts when he passes the ball: he may cut to the basket; he may cut to the ballside; or he may cut to the weakside.

- Back-Door Cuts

Any player at any position may cut any time that that player's defender makes a mistake. There are two types of cuts available: the back-door cut and the middle cut. To execute a back-door cut properly, the attacker wants to step in the direction of the ball before planting his outside foot, pushing off hard, taking a long step with his inside foot, and quickly racing toward the basket. The back-door cut is used when an offensive player's defender glances at the ball, taking his eyes off of the player.

The back-door cut should also be employed when a defender overplays his opponent when in a denial stance, especially when the defender's front knee extends over his front foot. Because this situation puts too much pressure on the denial, the offensive player can race back door before the defender can recover his balance.

We advocate and want the back-door cut used constantly, even sometimes when it is not there. Successful or not, the back-door cut can provide better spacing. Accordingly, we encourage any player at any position to use the back-door cut whenever he thinks he has the advantage. The back-door cut is covered more extensively in Chapter 9.

- Middle Cut

As a general rule, we want the middle cut used sparingly. A player should never use it when his middle cut will take him near the ball. All factors considered, it is not as good for the offense as the back-door cut. On occasion, however, its use may lead to a lay-up and a foul for a possible three-point play.

What is the middle cut? It is a cut between the offensive player's defender and the basketball. Subsequently, a pass to the cutter and a dribble drive usually ends in a three-point play because the defender is on the cutter's back and he cannot stop the cutter without coming over his back. When the cutter goes to shoot the lay-up, he wants to jump slightly into his defender, accentuating contact, gaining the foul call. It is essential that the cutter concentrate and make the lay-up.

When should the middle cut be used? The middle cut should be used whenever an offensive player's defender drops too far off of him toward the basket. A step away from the ball will usually get his defender stepping away from the ball. Following this step away with a dart toward the basket between his defender and the ball is the middle cut. An offensive player also wants to use the middle cut whenever his defender fails to jump toward the ball on each pass. In that case, which seldom happens in modern-day basketball, the defender is out of position, and an offensive player should take advantage of it. But never, never, never, should an offensive player use the middle cut when his defender has proper position toward the ball. That maneuver would only take him into the ball and take his team out of the motion offense. the middle cut is examined in more detail in Chapter 9.

•   Cut To the Basket WeakSide

Diagram 1-7 depicts the initial cut of the Five Man Open Post Motion Offense. 1 passes to 2. 1 must immediately read his defender and make a cutting decision. If the defender plays 1 properly, 1 can either cut to the basket or cut to replace himself.

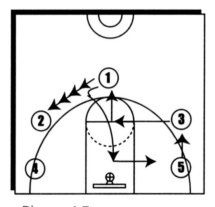

Diagram 1-7

Cutting to replace oneself should be used most infrequently because it is not an attacking cut. In Diagram 1-7, 1 decides to back-door cut to the basket. It should be kept in mind that 1 takes a step toward the pass receiver before planting and racing back door.

Once 1 commits himself to cut to the basket, 1 must go all the way to the basket before breaking out to the open spot (Rules to Replace). This tactic of going all the way to the basket opens up the remainder of the court for 1's teammates to maneuver. It also gives 1 one last change to maneuver for a pass and a lay-up. If X1 does not cover 1 correctly (Note: while the defense is left out of the diagram, X1 covers 1, X2 guards 2, X3 defends 3, etc. throughout this book), 1 can reverse pivot and put X1 on his back. A pass inside to the posting 1 should get the lay-up and a possible three-point play.

To secure the proper posting position, 1 should place his body near his defender's body just prior to the posting technique. When 1 sees he has maneuvered X1 to a spot where X1 cannot see both his man and the ball on defense, 1 has the advantage. If X1 should glance at the ball, taking his eye off of 1, 1 should plant his inside foot as his pivot foot, and reverse pivot, making contact with X1. 1 should flair his left arm (in Diagram 1-7) out into X1's torso. His left arm should be used as leverage to keep X1 from getting back into a proper defensive position. 1 should raise his right arm, with his palms facing the ball and, his fingers spread, signaling for 2 to pass the ball inside to 1.

If X1 takes his eyes off the ball and looks at 1, 1 should take a step or two toward X1. In response, X1 may step away from the cutting 1, hoping to regain his vision of both his man and the ball. 1 should then pivot off his right foot, making contact with X1. 1 should again use his left arm as leverage and his right palm and his fingers spread as a target for 2 to pass the ball. This pass might even be a semi-lob. If it were a semi-lob, 1 should hold his floor position until the ball is directly over his head. 1 should then move toward the basket, receive the pass, and go up with the ball without ever bringing the ball down. This posting maneuvering by 1 must be a split-second occurrence. Once 1 commits to cut toward the basket, he must go all the way to the basket and must be willing to get out of the lane in a hurry.

3 now makes the next movement in the basic pattern of the cut to the basket (Diagram 1-7). 3 must fill 1's open spot (Rules to Replace). 3 must execute properly. 3 begins his cut just as 1 clears the free-throw line area. 3 breaks directly toward the ball. 3 is reading his defender as he cuts. If X3 overplays 3 or is in any type of denial position, 3 should use his back-door cut to the basket for a pass and a lay-up. Again, this pass might even be a semi lob. Of course, if 3 has out maneuvered X3, 3 can post up X3. 2 must be aware of the five-second count if 3 is trying to post up X3. If X3 is below the line between 3 and 2, then 3 plants his left foot, pushes hard with a wider right-foot slide to 1's vacated spot (Diagram 1-7). This maneuver gives 2 an opportunity to pass to 3 without fear of X3 intercepting the ball. 5 sees 3's spot empty and moves up to fill that spot, per the Rules of Replace. 1 now has to replace 5's void.

This entire pattern is called the basic cut to the basket, weakside (Diagram 1-7). As the diagram shows, 1 finally cuts weakside. An option also exists for 1 to cut strongside. That particular option is discussed in the next section.

• Cut To the Basket StrongSide

1 again passes to 2 and cuts to the basket. But while 1 is cutting to the basket, the strongside corner, 4, decides to run his curl and cuts up the side post to the high post (Diagram 1-8). The strongside corner may run this cut at his discretion. This maneuver is called cut to the basket strongside.

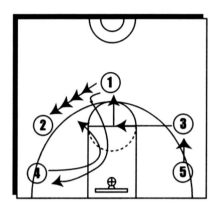

Diagram 1-8

To execute the side-post curl cut, the strongside corner walks his defender into the area just above the big block. If an opportunity occurs at any time to post, 4 takes advantage of that defensive lapse. 4 slides up the side post to an area around the high post. 4 is now available for two-on-two plays with 2 (refer to Chapter 9 for a discussion of two-on-two plays), for three-on-three plays with either 2 and 3, or with 2 and 1, (refer to Chapter 10 for an overview of three-on-three plays); or for screening maneuvers, including the staggered-screen series.

4 can stay at the low post while 3 flashes across the lane toward 2, and 5 fills for 3. 1 now has the choice of cutting either to the strongside or the weakside. In Diagram 1-8, 1 cuts to the basket, then cuts strongside. This option is very effective against zones, the match-up, or half-court traps (refer to Chapter 12 for details).

Cut To the Ball

The three major cutting maneuvers are cut to the basket, cut to the ball, and cut away from the ball. Cut-to-the-basket basic movements were discussed in the previous two sections. The various options for these movements are presented in Chapter 3. All the two- and three-player plays will be discussed in Chapters 9 and 10.

The second major basic cutting maneuver is the cut-to-the-ball pattern. Diagram 1-9 shows 1 passing to 2 and cutting to 2. 1 can either cut outside 2 for a pass back or he can cut inside 2 for a hand-off pass. 1 must read the way X2 is playing 2 to determine which cut would be most beneficial. There are a number of two-player plays which can be operated from either cut. They are presented in Chapter 4. The drills used to perfect the execution of two-player plays are discussed in Chapter 9.

4 has a choice of staying in the corner when 1 activates the cut-to-the-ball options. 4 also has the freedom to run the side-post curl. The side-post curl enables 1 and 2

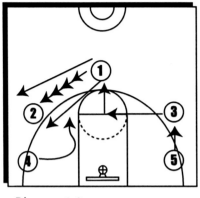

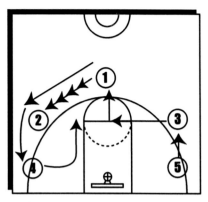

Diagram 1-9   Diagram 1-10

to operate their two-player plays to the outside, while 4—replacing himself—would grant 1 and 2 enough territory around the key to play their two-player games. Another advantage of 4 using the side-post curl is that it puts 4 into all two- and three-player games that 1 and 2 wish to activate. (Note: see Chapters 9 and 10 for the numerous options).

Diagram 1-10 illustrates 1 passing to 2 and cutting to the outside, but not getting a pass back from 2. In this instance, 1 has now cut to the corner where 4 began. 2 and 4 can run two-player plays. 2, 3, and 4 can run three-player plays, including all types of screening plays. These possibilities are examined in more detail in Chapter 4 and drilled on in Chapters 9 and 10. This is another excellent option against zones, the match-up, and half-court traps—especially when 4 stays at the low post.

Cut Away From The Ball

The last of the three major cutting options is to cut away from the ball. A number of effective three-player plays can be run as a result of this particular cutting maneuver. For example, in Diagram 1-11, 1 passes to 2 and cuts away to screen for 3. 3 sets up the screen by first moving away from 1 then coming back over 1's screen. 1 rolls to the basket. 2 must read the way the defenders X1 and X3 play this screen. Either 1 or 3 will become the primary receiver, while the other attacker will become the secondary receiver. The way 2 reads this defense and the details that make the screen-and-roll work are in discussed Chapter 10.

4 again has the freedom to replace himself or to run the side-post curl. If 4 replaces himself, the screen-and-roll between 1 and 3 not only fills the vacant spots (Rules to Replace), but the area inside the lane is open for the jumper by 3 or the lay-up by 1 (Diagram 1-11). The key point is that 2 must make the proper choice. On the other hand, that is why we perform drills—to perfect execution.

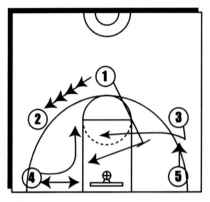

Diagram 1-11

If 4 chooses to run the side-post curl, 3 replaces 1 in his spot, and 1 either replaces the spot vacated by 4 or the corner spot once occupied by 5. 5 replaces 3's void, per the Rules to Replace. 4 is now in a position to join 2 and 3 in two-player or three-player games, or he can join 1 and 2 in two- or three-player schemes.

Summary

This chapter was designed to show you the three basic options: cut to the basket, cut to the ball, cut away from the ball. Each of the three basic movement patterns have chapters devoted solely to them. In Chapter 3, all the options of cutting to the basket are outlined. In Chapter 4, the choices associated with cutting to the ball are examined in detail. Finally, Chapter 5 presents all the alternatives available when 1 cuts away from the ball. Suggestions on how to drill each of those possibilities so that their execution can be perfected are then presented in Chapters 9 and 10. These chapters offer many of the numerous details necessary to teach the Five Man Open Post Motion Offense. Several useful offensive options and strategies are available, however, before the cutting maneuvers begin. These options and strategies are discussed in the next chapter.

2

Offense Before Cuts Begin

Several plays are available before 1 begins the basic movement with his pass and choice of cuts. One option we like strongly is the back-door cut. Any player who feels his defender has committed an error is free to back door his defender at any moment. A realistic opportunity exists for the middle cut when the defender has sagged too far off his assignment. Although the back-door cut is preferred, the middle cut is allowed. The other players operate under the Rules of Replace.

Freedom To Cut

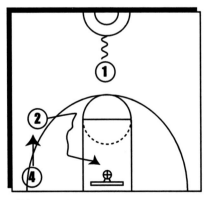

Diagram 2-1

Diagram 2-1 illustrates how the back-door and middle cuts work. As 1 is bringing the ball into the scoring area, 2 feels he can properly execute the back-door cut. 2 steps toward the dribbling 1, then back doors X2. 1 should hit him with the pass for the lay-up, if he can. 4 fills per Rules To Replace. If a corner player back doors (or middle cuts) before 1 has passed and cut, the corners should replace themselves. We don't want the wings replacing down. That is not one of the Rules To Replace.

Wings Screen Down

While 1 is dribbling the ball into the scoring area, the wings have the freedom to screen down for the corner players. Any time a screen is set, the screener is required to call the player's name for whom he is going to set the screen. The screener should raise his fist to let the receiver of the screen know he is calling the screen. Less mistakes are made if both a visual and an audio signal are used. Diagram 2-2 demonstrates 2 setting a screen for 4. 4 moves toward the baseline to set his defender up for the screen. 2 sets the screen and then rolls. If 1 cannot hit either 2 or 4 for a quick score, 4 should fill 2's spot, and 2 should replace 4.

Diagram 2-3 exhibits the flex cut. 2 back doors X2, then cuts back out to screen for the corner (4). 4 sets up X4 by moving high a step or two, then cutting back door. 2 rolls back into the lane for a possible post up. If there is no attempt to get the quick score; 2 pops back to his original position, and 4 goes back to the corner. These two maneuvers offer an excellent beginning movement against teams that try to deny the pass into the wing. This movement compels the defense to cover potential scoring maneuvers. All factors considered,while concentrating on that coverage, the defense cannot be in its best denial stance. The flex cut shown in Diagram 2-2 is also very good against sagging defenses. Putting a shooter at the 4 slot and a big screener at the 2 spot has the potential to enable the ofense to reap substantial rewards against a sagging defense.

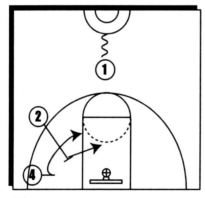

Diagram 2-2

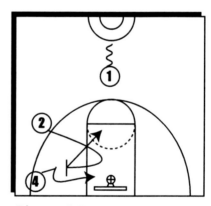

Diagram 2-3

Shuffle Cuts

As 1 is dribbling the basketball into scoring range, 4 runs his side-post curl. Upon seeing this, 2 sets his defender up for a shuffle cut off of 4's screen. Diagram 2-4 shows 2 cutting over the top of 4's screen, trying to achieve the same effect as a middle cut. Diagram 2-5 illustrates 2 breaking beneath 4's screen, displaying the back-door cut off of a shuffle screen. In both cases, 4 rolls back toward the ball. 1 then passes to 4, with 1 cutting off 4. This movement, termed the pinch-the-post technique (refer to pages 25-26 for a discussion of this technique), is a virtually unstoppable tactic when executed properly.

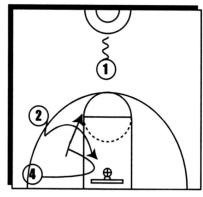

Diagram 2-4

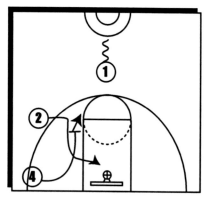

Diagram 2-5

Split The Flash Pivot

If a team has an excellent passing corner player, it might wish to employ a split-the-post, off-the-side-post curl. In Diagram 2-6, 1 is bringing the ball down the floor when 4 makes the side-post curl cut. 1 passes the ball to 4, and then goes to set the screen for 2, calling out 2's name and showing his fist. 2 dips away from the impending screen to set his defender, X2, up for the screen. Once 1 sets the screen, he rolls to the basket.

Diagram 2-6

If the defenders don't switch, 2 should have either a jump shot around the key area or a driving lay-up if his defender really trails him. 4 can help get 2 open by using the pinch-the-post technique. If a switch occurs, 1 should immediately reverse pivot, impelling X2 to get on 1's back. 1 then rolls to the basket, as in the middle cut (keeping X2 on his back) for the lay-up and possible three-point play.

Side-Post Curl with Back Door

Most defensive teams in modern basketball deny the wings the pass from the point to the wing. When this situation happens, it opens up all kinds of back-door tactics. In this regard, one of the most effective is the side-post curl with a back door. 4 executes his side-post curl. 1 passes 4 the ball. 2 immediately steps toward the cutting 4, plants his left foot hard, takes a long step with his right foot, and darts back door. 4 sits down as he receives the pass from 1. He then twists at the belt and tosses a soft bounce pass to the cutting 2.

Pinch The Post

One of the most unstoppable plays against a person-to-person defense is the pinch-the-post maneuver. Diagram 2-7 shows that the entire left side of the court has been cleared out when 2 broke back door.

If 3, not shown in the diagrams, is executing his weakside cut toward the free-throw line and 5 is filling the void left by 3's departure (per Rules of Replace), 2 can cut to the basket and then go on out to the right corner to take the spot 5 just vacated. This maneuver leaves the left side of the court completely open for the virtually unstoppable pinch-the-post.

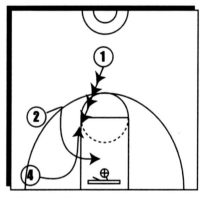

Diagram 2-7

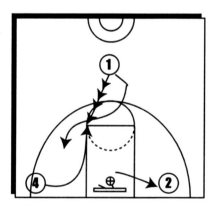

Diagram 2-8

Adherence to proper technique is extremely important in the pinch-the-post. 1 passes to 4, and then dips away from 4 as 2 finishes his back door cut (Diagram 2-8). 1 now runs directly at the full torso of 4, looking like he intends to run over 4. In reality, 1 intends to cut off of 4's right shoulder. As 1 gets to 4 (almost face to face, chest to chest), he reverse pivots. At this point, facing the basket, 4 reads the defense.

If 1 has executed correctly, X1 ran into 4, and is on 4's back. 4 is facing the basket, reading how X4 intends to play the cutting 1. If X4 stays with 4, 4 hands off to 1, who then drives for the lay-up. If X4 is faking going to 1 and jumping back, 4 just allows 1 to cut toward the basket. He then tosses 1 the ball for a lay-up. If X4 switches off onto 1, 4 takes one dribble, pushing the ball out in front of himself so X1 cannot deflect it and lays the ball in the basket. It is important to remember that X1 is on 4's back. If 4 made a mistake and handed the ball off to 1 while X4 was actually covering 1, he drives toward the basket for a return pass from 1 and a lay-up. When executed properly, the pinch-the-post is virtually unstoppable. The actual clearout by 2 allows 1 and 4 to operate any of the two-player plays that are discussed in Chapter 9. This tactic is excellent when a team has its two best players in the 1 and the 4 slots.

Summary

The heart of the Five Player Open Post Motion Offense is the three basic cutting movements by 1: cut to the basket, cut to the ball, cut away from the ball. This chapter presented several movements that could occur before 1 gets the offense going.

3

Cut-to-the-Basket Options

In Chapter 1, Diagrams 1-7 and 1-8 illustrated the cut to the basket weakside and strongside basic motion. A better understanding of the diagrams that are presented in this chapter can be gained by reviewing those diagrams..

As you recall, 1 passes and cuts to the basket. Upon seeing 1 cut to the basket, the weakside wing (3 in the diagrams) immediately breaks along the direct line to 2. 4, at the same moment, has the option to stay where he is, to replace himself with a V cut, or to run the side-post curl pattern. These maneuvers open up many options for the players to use in the cut-to-the-basket series. In fact, the cut-to-the-basket series can be taught as a complete offense in itself, if time is an element in a team's season preparation. This chapter presents the various options that are available in the cut-to-the-basket series.

The Initial Cut

1 passes to 2 in Diagram 3-1. X1 jumps to the ball, which is the proper defensive technique. 1 reads this movement by his defender and steps in the direction that X1 jumped in the hopes that he can decoy X1 into moving even further toward 2. 1 plants his right foot, pushes off hard, takes a longer step with his left foot, and darts toward the basket. If the back-door pass is there, 2 should throw it. It should result in a lay-up. If the lob pass is there, 2 should deliver it. 1 should catch the lob pass and keep the

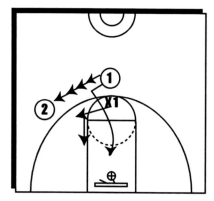

Diagram 3-1

ball up. 1 can lay the ball in if the pass is around the rim while he is still in the air. Under no circumstances should 1 bring the ball down below chin level before exploding back up for the lay-up. Pump fakes may be used if necessary.

The back-door cut offers at least two advantages. First, most teams play jump-to-the-ball defense, and their defenders tend to make relatively few mistakes. In that regard, if a team consistently makes the defensive mistake of not jumping to the ball, it will probably be defeated anyway. Second, a team doesn't want its offense confused by 1 moving too close to the ball receiver. It makes it look like the cut-to-the-ball series.

X1 does not jump to the ball in Diagram 3-2. Instead, X1 drops to the basket. 1 steps away from his pass to 2, hoping to convince X1 to move even another step away from 2. When this occurs, 1 plants hard on his left foot, extends his right foot a little longer, and darts down the lane between his defender and the ball. This maneuver is called the middle cut. Because X1 is now on 1's back, a pass from 2 will get 1 the lay-up and possibly a 3-point play.

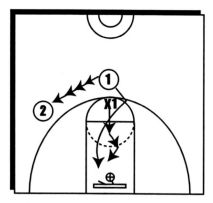

Diagram 3-2

1 can post up momentarily near the basket as he completes his cut. Diagram 3-3 shows 1 maneuvering X1 close enough to his body so that he can reverse pivot and seal X1 on his back. To accomplish this, 1 cuts to the basket, being ever mindful that at a certain point, X1 will not be able to see both him and the ball. When 1 has X1 at this disadvantage, he reads X1's coverage. If X1 drops too deep, X1 will be underneath the back board. This situation would allow 1 to flash back to the ball and easily post X1. If X1 moves more toward 2, the lob pass is a real possibility. As a result, X1 will most likely move toward 1. When this occurs, 1 should move to a position about a half step above X1. 1 should then reverse pivot and put his left arm out strong, hopefully into the torso of X1. 1 should then use slide steps to keep X1 sealed. A pass to 1 would then give him the lay-up.

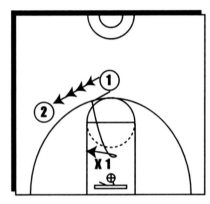

Diagram 3-3

Should none of these options occur, 1 must decide to exit the basket area. Keep in mind, these movements should be made rapidly. The basket area should never be clogged. 1's teammates are moving while his cut is occurring, and they may have the opportunity to cut to the basket for a score. Accordingly, 1's movement must be quick, but not fast. 1's last decision is whether to cut weakside or strongside. 1 knows from the Rules To Replace that the weakside area is open. But if 4 has opted to use the side-post curl, then the strongside is also open, per the Rules To Replace.

The success of 1's initial cut is affected by his read of his defender. If 1 reads well, the team scores, and there is no second option. Should the defense be sound, 1's teammates have read that 1 is running the cut-to-the-basket series, and have already begun their cuts.

WeakSide Wing Cut

It is most important that 3 begins his cut as 1 clears the area of the free-throw line. Equally as important, 3's cut must be directly toward 2 who has the basketball. This direct cut toward 2 can put an essentially sound defense at a disadvantage. Diagram 3-4 shows X3 in perfect denial defense. Reading the situation, 3 plants his right foot, pushes hard, takes a little longer step with his left foot, and back-door cuts X3. 1 has cleared the area. 5, not shown in Diagram 3-4, is filling 3's spot per the Rules of Replace.

X3 has sagged off of 3 as 3 is making his cut. X3 has jumped to the ball on the initial pass and is slowly dropping toward the basket. 3 reads this and opts to replace 1, an action that is really 3's intentions, per the Rules To Replace. This maneuver allows 2 to reverse the ball without fear of it being intercepted.

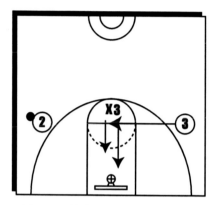

Diagram 3-4

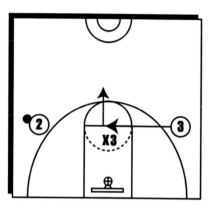

Diagram 3-5

Diagram 3-6 shows that X3 has made the classic defensive mistake. Instead of jumping to the ball, X3 sagged toward the basket on 1's initial pass to 2. 3 reads this misplay and cuts between X3 and the ball. 3 has X3 on his back. A pass from 2 can easily result in a three-point play. In reality, such a display by 3 occurs infrequently because most teams are well drilled on defense. It does happen, however. As a result, a coach should ensure that his players are aware of its possibility.

Two other possibilities exist from such a weakside cut by 3. 3 can get his defender into a spot where X3 cannot see both his man and the ball. 3 can then reverse pivot and post X3 in the same manner as 1 posted X1 on his initial cut. The other possibility involves 5, who is now replacing 3, who is cutting to the basket. As 5 begins to replace the original spot of 1, 5 now has the same options as 3 had on the weakside cut.

The aforementioned are the major cutting options of the cut-to-the-basket series. 4, however, can run his side-post curl at his discretion. This action opens up many more opportunities for the cut-to-the-basket series. The remainder of this chapter is devoted to 4's side-post curl and other staggered screening options.

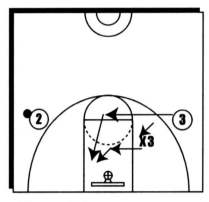

Diagram 3-6

Swing and Go

As 1 cuts to the basket, he sees 4 exercising his option to run his side-post curl. A good part play is for 4 to stop at the low post and allow 1 to rub his defender off on 4 (an old Cincinnati swing-and-go tactic used in the 1960's to win two consecutive national championships).

Diagram 3-7 depicts this swing-and-go scheme. 1 tries to get X1 to trail him around the stationary screen set by 4. 4 can help this maneuver by moving somewhat himself. 4 must, however, be alert not to set a moving screen.

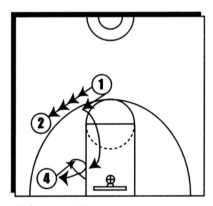

Diagram 3-7

1 and 2 should read X1's coverage to make the best cut and to pick the best time to pass inside to 1. Should 1 get a pass inside, 4 should roll to the basket, giving a target hand for a possible return pass. If 1 does not get the pass, he should continue on out to the corner after his full circle. 2 and 1 can now pass the ball to each other as 4 tries to get his defender posted. If this does not happen shortly, 4 moves on up

to the side post in his curl or even to the high post. 2 can reverse the ball to 3, who replaced 1 and 2. Then 3 and 4 can run a three-player game (refer to Chapter 10 for three-player drills).

Because the situation involves tight quarters with inside passing a premium, 4 wants to face 1, once 1 gets the pass from 2. 4 can use either reverse or front pivots to try to get X1 rubbed off of 1. But once 1 gets the ball, 4 should quickly turn to face 1, roll to the basket, and give a target hand. Because of the tight quarters, X4 often helps 4 screen X1.

An alternative is for 1 to begin his cut to the basket, but call out 4's name, signifying that he wants 4 to use him for a screen. 1 should also hold up his fist. In Diagram 3-8, 1 stops at the low post. 4 then begins his side post-curl pattern.

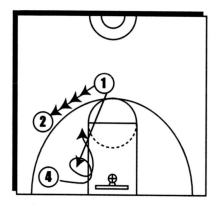

Diagram 3-8

4, however, has the option to use 1 as a swing-and-go partner before cutting out to the high post. 1 should then fill in 4's slot. 4 and 2 should read X4's coverage for the best place to cut and the best time to pass the ball inside. Should 4 get a pass inside, 1 should roll to the basket with a target hand up for a return pass. If something does not develop quickly, 2 can reverse the ball to 3. At this point, 2, 3, and 4 again make use of a three-player game.

Staggered and Optional Screens

1 and 4 can pair to set either staggered or optional screens for 2. If 2 is an exceptional shooter off of the dribble, the following plays can be very effective. 1 passes to 2 and begins his cut to the basket. However, either before 1 passes to 2 or as 1 is passing to 2, 4 decides to use his side-post curl. When 1 sees 4's curl, he stops near the free-throw line and sets a staggered screen. 4 will have set the other stagger screen outside the lane at the high post (Diagram 3-9).

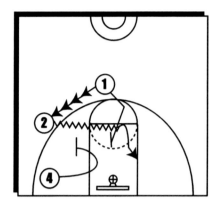

Diagram 3-9

2 fakes first to his right before beginning his dribble to his left. 2 tries to rub X2 off on 4's shoulder. If X4 switches, 2 continues to try to rub X4 off on 1's shoulder. If X1 switches, 1 rolls to the basket for a possible pass back. If X1 calls the switch too quickly, 1 rolls for an immediate pass and a lay-up. 2 reads the defense as he dribbles. 2 has the option of stopping and shooting the jumper at any time a defensive miscue occurs.

Diagram 3-10 demonstrates another way to get into the staggered screen. 3 cuts across the lane to begin his filling for 1's void, per Rules To Replace. 3, however, does not break either outside or back door. Instead, 3 sets a screen. Meanwhile, 1 stops his cut to the basket short and comes to the side-high post to set a screen for 2. 3 will know this, because 1 will be showing a fist and calling 2's name.

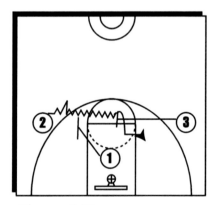

Diagram 3-10

A third method to get a staggered screen would be for 1 to continue his cut to the basket and out either the weakside or strongside. Meanwhile, 3 comes to the middle of the lane to set a screen, because he heard and saw 4 running his side-post curl and calling 2's name. As a result, 4 sets the staggered screen just outside the lane, while 3 sets the second part of the screen in the middle of the key. (Note: a diagram to depict this method is not included in this section.)

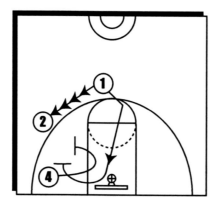

Diagram 3-11

Diagram 3-11 illustrates a method of setting optional screens. 1 passes to 2 and cuts all the way to the basket before starting to replace 4 in the corner. 4 has meanwhile ran his side-post curl option. 4 sets a high post screen for 2; and 1 sets a screen just outside of the lane near the second lane marking for 2.

2, who must be able to shoot off of the dribble, has the option of using whichever screen is best for him. 2 reads X2. If X2 is playing straight between 2 and the line to the basket, 2 should fake one direction or the other with a rocker step move before beginning his dribble in the opposite direction. If X2 is overplaying either left or right, 2 should rocker step in the direction of the overplay and then begin his dribble in the opposite direction. The screener can either be facing 2 or playing with his back to 2. 2 drives directly toward the screener, rubbing X2 off on the screener's shoulder. 2 now can either continue for the lay-up or can pull up for the jump shot. The screener rolls to the basket for a possible pass, giving a target with one of his hands. Also, the roll gives the screener a great opportunity for an offensive rebound if there has been a switch.

Both the stagger screen and the optional screen are very good plays for the last shot of any quarter of the ball game. The ball is in the hands of a team's best scorer. Because a team is running a play that is has undoubtedly practiced and drilled on many, many times, the play's chances of success are very high.

Reversal Patterns

The cut-to-the-basket series is not finished when the ball is reversed. At this point, the reversal just signifies that the ball is put into the hands of 3, who has filled 1's void, per the Rules of Replace. Many scoring opportunities are immediately available to 3 before he signals cut-to-the-basket, cut-to-the-ball, or cut-away-from-the-ball series by his pass and movement.

1 has passed to 2, cut to the basket, and filled the space left vacant by 5. 5 has filled the void of 3. 3 has replaced 1. All of these moves are dictated by the Rules of Replace. Upon the pass to 3 from 2, 5 slides to the high post at the side of the key. 1, seeing and hearing 5's screening maneuver, decides to make it a stagger screen by moving slightly outside the lane into a wing spot (Diagram 3-12). 3 can now use the staggered screen for a jump shot, drive to basket, or pass back to the rolling 1. 3 reads the defense as he dribbles to his left.

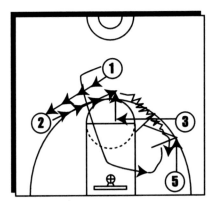

Diagram 3-12

Duck-In Tactic

Diagram 3-13 shows 1 ducking back into the lane after completing his cut to the basket. Seeing the pass being reversed, 1 realizes that he can gain an advantage on X1 by ducking back into the basket and getting a post-up position for the high-low sequence. The key is 1's read of X1.

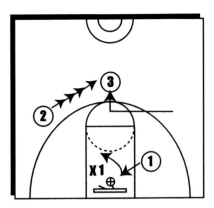

Diagram 3-13

High-Post Screen For The Cut

1 is being pressured by X1 as he dribbles the ball into the front court. Having seen 4 running the side-post curl, 1 has heard 4 calling his name. 1 knows that a high-post screen will be set for him at the free-throw line. 1 passes to 2, sets X1 up by dipping away from the screen, and then breaks hard off of the shoulder of 4 (Diagram 3-14). 2 is also aware that this screen is developing. He can hear 1's name being called and see 4's fist in the air.

Diagram 3-14

Summary

The cut to the basket and the weakside wing cut are the two basic maneuvers of the cut-to-the-basket series. The swing and go, the staggered and optional screens, the reversal patterns, and the duck-in tactic are other options that enable a team to take advantage of its personnel, as well as create an offense using only the cut-to-the-basket series. A team can begin the season with only the basic movements of the Five Player Open Post Motion Offense and add any of the aforementioned options as the season progresses.

In the next chapter, the cut-to-ball series is discussed in deatail. Combining the cut-to-ball series with the cut-to-basket series can give a team a very well-rounded offense.

4

Cut-to-the-Ball Options

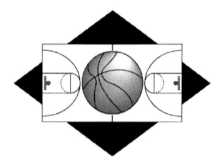

In our nomenclature, there are two cuts to the ball: outside and inside. 1 passes the ball, fakes away from the ball (or to basket), and then comes back to the ball. 1 now has the choice of going either outside of 2 or inside of 2. A team can score from either option. The outside cut to the ball is discussed first.

Go Outside & Return Of Ball

The first step in cutting to the ball is being able to get the ball back from the pass receiver. Diagram 4-1 illustrates a technique that has traditionally been very successful.

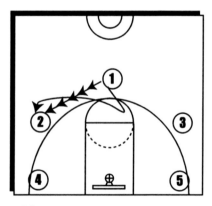

Diagram 4-1

In Diagram 4-1, 1 passes the ball to 2 and cuts to the ball to get the ball back. If 2 is close enough to the basket when 1 passes him the ball to him, a return pass to 1 will allow 1 to get a three-point shot off over the screening 2. If 2 keeps the ball, no danger exists in the ball being turned over. On the other hand, if 2 hands the ball back to 1, an errant hand off is a real possibility.

When cutting to the ball, 1 should first set his defender up by faking a cut away from the ball or faking a cut to the basket. 2 should return the ball to 1 off his left hip while still facing the basket. Upon getting the ball back from 2, 1 should have his shoulders squared to the basket in a triple-threat position. As a result, 1 can shoot, drive, or pass without having to reset the basketball.

Go Outside & Drive Off Of 2's Screen

In Diagram 4-2, 1 passes the ball to 2, cuts to the ball, and receives the pass back from 2. If he does not feel that the shot is immediately available, 1 begins to look for the drive. 1 must read the defense (Diagram 4-2). If X1 offers defensive pressure from the right side of his teammate (2), 1 should drive left. If the defensive pressure comes from the left side of 2, he should drive right. 2 should pin 1's defensive man by stepping through with his inside foot. This action will immediately create a two-on-one situation where a team can attack the basket. 2 will roll to the basket as 1 drives (refer to Chapter 10 for proper screen-and-roll mechanics). 2 will be open more often than 1 because a switch almost always occurs.

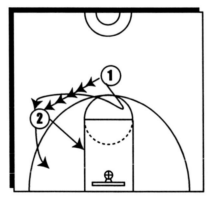

Diagram 4-2

This tactic will almost always work when X1 sags behind 2, trying to anticipate which direction 1 intends to drive. 2's step through screen will prevent X1 from getting to 1's drive. However, unless X2 switches to 1, 1 will have the driving lay-up. On the other hand, if X2 switches to 1, 2 will have X1 on his back as 2 rolls to the basket.

Go Outside & Defense Fights Over Top

When X1 gets overly aggressive, or when it is the nature of the defensive team for X1 to fight over the top, 1 should continue his cut to the corner. 2 should easily be able to pick X1, using the techniques described in Chapter 2 on the pinch the post technique.

In Diagram 4-3, 1 goes outside of 2, and 2 picks X1. When this tactic is executed properly, 1 and 2 have a two-on-one situation going to the basket. If 2 has handed the ball off to 1, X2 must switch or 1 will drive for the lay-up. If X2 does switch, then 2 has X1 on his back. Either way, 1 or 2 will have a lay-up attempt. If 2 misjudged the defense, 1 continues his cut on toward the basket. If 2 has indeed screened X1, but 2 did not give 1 the ball, X2 often stays with 2. If 1 continues his cut to the basket, 1 will get a pass back from 2 for the lay-up. If 2 pins X1, and X2 switches to 1 on his cut to the basket, 2 has a drive for the lay-up. (Note: this tactic is the same technique as the pinch the post.)

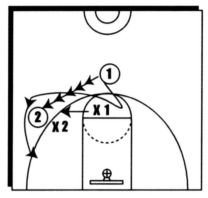

Diagram 4-3

Go Inside & Hand Ball Off

Go inside is our terminology for the passer to cut inside the pass receiver for a hand off. All factors considered, this tactic is most effective when the defender on the pass receiver sags off of the receiver. In Diagram 4-4, 1 passes to 2 and cuts inside 2 because X2 is not in denial stance on 2. 2 is also outside shooting range. As 1 makes his inside cut, 1 begins reading the defense. If the defense is playing in a regular defensive position (i.e., not denial and not a sag), then 1 should screen X2 (Diagram 4-4). 1 should roll to the basket. A description and details of executing the screen-and-roll tactic are presented in Chapter 10.

If the defense calls "switch" before the screen is set, 1 "splits the switch" (Diagram 4-5). To achieve this "split of the switch," 1 simply plants his right foot, pushes off hard, faces the end line, raises his left hand as a target, and cuts sharply to the basket. This

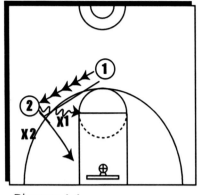

Diagram 4-4   Diagram 4-5

tactic leaves X2 behind. 2 can then toss a semi-lob pass to 1 for the lay-up. It also leaves X1 a half step behind 2. 2 could either dribble to his right for the easy jump shot or drive for a lay-up.

If 1 approaches 2, and X2 sags because he does not think 2 is a threat to shoot the ball, 1 cuts between X2 and 2 to receive a hand-off pass (Diagram 4-6). At this point, 1 really has two defenders. When X2 sees 1 get the ball, and 1 begins to dribble hard toward the basket, X2 will usually try to defend the ball. X1, who stayed with 1 all the way, will usually continue to cover 1. 2 then breaks in the direction opposite 1's dribble for a possible pass back and an easy jump shot or drive. On numerous occasions, X2 will screen X1 if the hand off is not seen quickly by X2. Because X2 does not expect the hand-off pass, he cannot afford to open up more than he already has sagged. If 1 reads the sag by X2 correctly, this option offers an excellent opportunity to score.

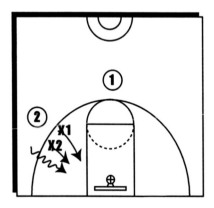

Diagram 4-6

Diagrams 4-1 through 4-6 show several options for cutting to the ball. Three of those options involve cutting outside the receiver, while three involve cutting *inside* the receiver. At this point, other alternatives that are available to these two players when 1 chooses to cut to the ball should also be considered.

Screening The Receiver

In Diagram 4-7, 1 cuts to the ball, not intending to receive an inside hand off, but continuing past X2 to set the screen. Usually both X2 and X1 will stay on the same side of the screen, giving 2 a driving lay-up to his right or at least a wide-open jump shot behind the screen. Should X2 see what is occurring and call the "switch" prematurely, 1 should "split the screen" for a pass back from 2.

To execute this tactic properly, 1 should cut by X2 with his hands out as though he expects 2 to hand him the ball. One step beyond X2, 1 pivots on his right foot and faces X2 with a screen. As a rule, X1 stays on the same side of 1 as X2 because that would be his proper defensive position if no switch has been called. As a result, both X1 and X2 get caught on the high side of 1's screen. 1 must read the defense correctly and oversell his cut, making X2 and X1 think a hand off is about to occur. This option is best utilized after running several plays that employ an inside cut with a hand-off pass.

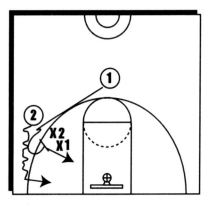

Diagram 4-7

In modern basketball, many team defenses subscribe to the sagging theory, in the belief that they do not have to worry about helping defense. When a team runs up against an opponent that sags excessively on defense, it can get great jump shots by screening for the pass receiver. Diagram 4-8 displays this attacking tactic. 1 cuts toward the ball and screens down on the sagging X2. 2 can dribble in behind 1's screen for the uncontested jump shot.

As a point of emphasis, a team should want to bury the defense as deep as a defensive team will allow. Often, defenders are taught to *exaggerate a slough* sag too far. A few passes before exercising the screen down can result in the defense sagging too deeply.

Dribble Entries

On occasion, 2 is overplayed by a very skilled defender. Rather than let that defender throw off the timing of its offense, a team should just activate dribbling entries into the offense.

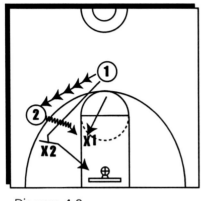

Diagram 4-8

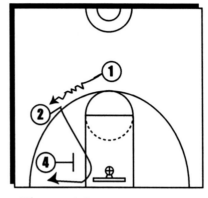

Diagram 4-9

For example, 1 dribbles toward 2 (Diagram 4-9). 2 sees the dribbling entry and knows that he is being overplayed. Accordingly, 2 reads X2, steps toward the dribbling 1, hoping to get X2 out on his toes, and cuts back door. Reading the move by 1 and 2, 4 begins his side-post curl but stops at the low post to set a screen for 2. This pattern is a very good offensive play against sagging zone defenses. Three other dribble-entry possibilities are shown in Diagrams 4-10, 4-11, and 4-12. Innumerable other alternatives exist. The point to remember is that a team should select its options based upon its available personnel during a particular year.

In order for the options presented in Diagrams 4-10, 4-11, and 4-12 to be successful, 1 must read X2 properly. In Diagram 4-10, 1 dribbles toward 2. 2 dips, setting his defender up for the upcoming screen. 1 sets the screen on the high side of X2, compelling X2 to go beneath the screen. 1 hands off to 2. 1 rolls to the basket after the hand off. 2 has the option of shooting the jump shot, dribbling for a better shot, or returning the pass to the cutting 1.

Diagram 4-10

Diagram 4-11

In Diagram 4-11, 1 continues his dribble past X2. Because he is anticipating the screen, X2 is not fully aware of 2's cut. As a consequence, X2 might even call for a premature "switch". 2 then cuts behind 1 as 1 is dribbling. 1 can hand off to 2, or he can continue his dribble. If X2 is late on his coverage, 1 hands off to 2. If X2 quickly scurries past 1 to get back on 2, 1 keeps his dribble alive and allows 2 to cut to the basket.

In Diagram 4-12, X2 is overplaying 2. 2 dips and cuts back door. Seeing this, 4 runs his side-post curl pattern. This action clears the entire outside of the court for the back-door cut of 2. 1 can either keep his dribble alive and use 4's side-post position to execute a screen and roll with 4 or pass to 4 and run the pinch-the-post strategy.

Diagram 4-12

Three-Player Plays and Other Options

Several movements are available for three players working inside the cut to the ball series, including using screens and using staggered screens. Even the weave is a possibility.

Diagram 4-13 shows 1 passing to 2, cutting to the ball, and getting the pass back from 2. Meanwhile, 4 runs his side-post curl pattern, ending up setting a back screen for 2 at the side high-post level. 1 can throw the lob pass to 2 if X4 does not switch onto the cutting 2. If X4 does switch, 2 circles back out to the corner to fill the void of 4's cut per the Rules To Replace. As X4 switches, 4 pins X2 onto his back, allowing 1 to toss the lob pass to 4.

If X2 manages to get over the top of 4's back screen, 4 can sit down in posting position to get the pass from 1 for a one-on-one power move inside. As an alternative, 1 and 4 can run the pinch-the-post maneuver.

Another alternative involves 2 cutting to the low post and looking for the pass from 1 in the low-post position. A pass to 4 from 1 would give 2 and 4 an opportunity to play the high-low post game (Diagram 4-14). Meanwhile, 1 could go to the low post to set a screen for 2 to pop around, activating the three-player game. At this point, 1 and 2 can either run the swing-and-go or read their defenders, allowing 2 to pop out

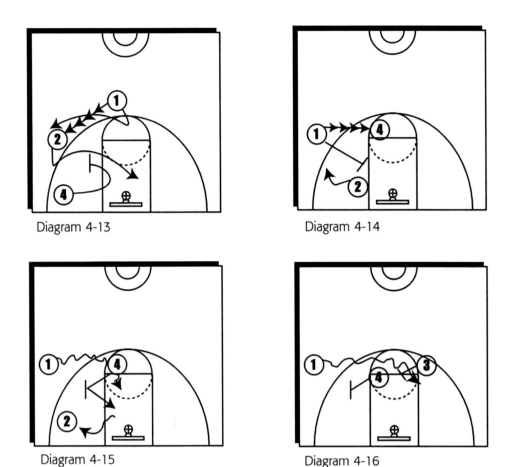

Diagram 4-13

Diagram 4-14

Diagram 4-15

Diagram 4-16

for the short jumper and 1 to roll to the basket to play the high-low post game with 4. Should 4 pass to 2 on the pop out the three-player movements are still not over. 1 could screen up for 4, or 4 could screen down for 1.

Additional continuations of the movements illustrated in Diagram 4-13 exist. Diagram 4-13 ends at the point where 1 has the ball, 4 has side-post curled to the high post, and 2 is cutting to the corner to fill 4's vacated spot. Diagram 4-15 shows 1 dribbling off of 4's high-post screen and roll. 1 and 4 then read the defense and use the option that comes open in the screen-and-roll maneuvers (see Chapter 10 for details).

As was discussed in Chapter 1, 3 begins his cut in a direct line toward 1 after 1 has passed the ball to 2 and cut to the ball. This maneuver allows 3 and 4 to set staggered screens for 1 to dribble off of (Diagram 4-16). This tactic is especially effective when facing a sagging X3 and X4.

The potential of 1 using a double screen when he uses the dribble entry into the wing exists. Diagram 4-17 depicts 1 dribbling toward 2. 2 is being overplayed. 4 runs his side-post curl. At this point, 2, the over-playing X2 and 4 provide a formidable screening pattern for 1 to drive over the top. Should X2 see this action coming and call the "switch", 2 could back-door cut X1 into the back screen of 4. If all this fails, 1 can pick up his dribble and pass to 4 running any of the options described in Diagram 4-16.

The dribbling weave is also a viable option. Diagram 4-18 shows 1 using the dribbling entry into the wing. This time, however, 1 dribbles to the inside of 2, setting a screen on X2. 1 is calling out 2's name and raising his fist. This action tells 2 to set up X2 by dipping away before coming to accept the screen. 1 then hands off to 2, who dribbles toward the middle of the court. 4 could even enter the picture by running his side-post curl. At this point, 4 is in perfect position to set a screen for the dribbling 2. 2 and 4 should play this as a screen and roll (the mechanics of which are described in detail in Chapter 10).

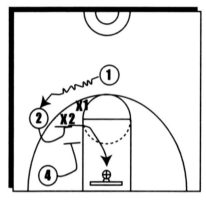
Diagram 4-17

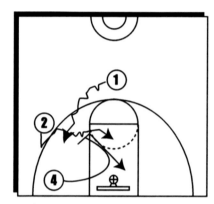
Diagram 4-18

Summary

At this point, the offense includes both a cut-to-the-basket series and a cut-to-the-ball series. Many options are given for each series. Either series can become an offense unto itself. Chapters 9 and 10 present drills that are designed to perfect the execution of any or all of the alternatives.

Chapter 5 introduces many possibilities that should be considered when using the third of the major offensive cuts—cut away from the ball. When a team employs all three of the major strategies, it will not only have an effective offense against a person-to-person defense, it will be in a position to defeat zones, match-ups, half court traps, and combination defenses. It will also have a stall, a delay game, and a last- shot offense.

5

Cut-Away-from-the-Ball Options

Cuts away from the ball can be used for a variety of purposes, including as a zone offense, a stall, as an attack versus the half-court trap, and as a tactic to counteract the match-up. These cuts can also be used to free up a particular individual for an easy jump shot or a one-on-one move.

Diagram 5-1 exhibits the basic screening away from the ball. This tactic can occur either at the weakside wing or at the weakside corner. In Diagram 5-1, 1 passes to 2 and then goes to screen for 3. 1 should immediately roll to the basket. 2 reads the defense of X1. If no switch occurs, the primary receiver is 3. If a switch happens, the primary receiver is 1. To execute the screen perfectly, 3 should dip away from the

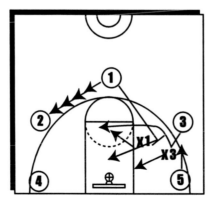

Diagram 5-1

screen to set up X3. 1 should get the proper angle to set the screen. 1 should set the screen on the upper half of X3. This action compels X3 to go beneath the screen. If X3 fights over the top of the screen, 3 would gain the advantage. In response to the fight-over-the-top defensive strategy, 3 should cut directly toward the basket for the middle cut and the lay-up. 1 would then be the jump shooter coming back toward the ball.

Just as X3 goes beneath 1's screen, 1 reverse pivots, making incidental contact with X3 and keeping X3 from a direct route to 3. X1 must either switch or concede 3 the uncontested shot. If X1 switches, X3 is on 1's back—resulting in a lay-up. 5 is filling the void created by 3's cut, per the Rules To Replace. 4 is replacing himself (or staying stationary). This tactic keeps their defenders busy and out of the play.

1 passes to 2 and goes to screen for 5. 1 can set either the down screen or the baseline screen. Diagram 5-2 shows the baseline screen being set. 5 breaks off the screen low, after setting X5 up for the screen. 1 curls back toward the ball. 2 again reads X1. If a switch happens, 1 is the primary receiver. If a switch does not occur, 5 is the primary receiver. Should 2 hit 1, 5 can easily seal X1 for the dump-down pass from 1. This tactic is the old weakside pin-down play made famous by the great UCLA teams under its renowned coach, John Wooden. Frequently, a three-point play results.

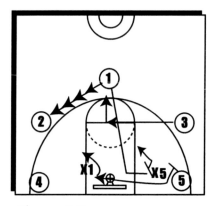

Diagram 5-2

3 is replacing 1, who left a vacancy at the point when he began his cut. 4 is replacing himself, or standing stationary. This tactic eliminates X3 and X4 from participating in help defense. Dips in the opposite direction of the screen should always occur. Not only does it set up the defender for the perfect angle for the screener, it enables all of the offensive players know where and when the screen is going to occur.

4 Can Become A Participant

Many plays are available that can be planned and still stay inside the framework of the Five Player Open Post Motion Offense. 4 can run his side-post curl. A pass to 4 can activate an entire new series of events using 1's screen away.

Diagram 5-3 demonstrates 4 running his side-post curl option. 1 passes to 4 and begins to screen away. 2 decides to defeat X2 by going back door. 4 checks this option first by turning his head to his left. If it is there, a bounce pass produces the lay-up. Concurrently, 1 has screened for 3. 4 reads X1 to see who the primary receiver is. 1 rolls to the basket. 4 can either hit 3 for the jump shot or can hit 1 for the lay-up. 5 is using the Rules To Replace to fill the void left by 3.

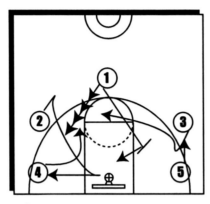

Diagram 5-3

Plans for the screening game should be based on a team's knowledge of how its opponents intend to play the screen and roll. If an opponent intends to switch the screen and roll, a team wants its big man setting the screens for its smaller players. Under that defensive scheme, a team's best jump shooters would be coming to the ball, and its biggest players would be rolling to the basket, usually with a smaller defender on them.

The point to remember is that a team's offensive scheme is not over with the screen and roll. 4 could either ignite the pinch-the-post with 3 or could initiate the weave (or dribbling screen) by dribbling toward 3 with the intent to hand the ball off to 3.

1 Initiates Shuffle Into Flex

Once a team begins drilling and using the offense, it will see that there are numerous variations that the players will develop in their cuts and choices. One such version is illustrated in Diagrams 5-4 and 5-5, which combines the shuffle cut into the flex offense. This option is just one among many that are available with a motion offense that allows a team's players freedom of choices, especially when the post is left open via the Five Players Open Post Motion Offense.

Diagram 5-4 depicts 1 passing to 2 and cutting away from the ball. 1 stops around the mid-post area and sets a back-door screen for 3. 3 dips and uses the screen as a shuffle cut. 1 comes back to the ball. 2 checks X1 to see who the primary receiver will be. 5 is running his Rules To Replace.

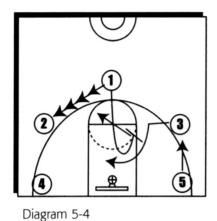

Diagram 5-4

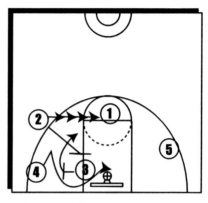

Diagram 5-5

Diagram 5-5 shows the pass being made back to 1 from 2. 4 dips and employs 3's screen at the low post. 2 goes to screen down for 3. If 2 then replaces 4's corner position, the offense is in the flex motion.

Summary

A team has a choice of several offensive cutting movements, including cut to the basket, cut to the ball, or cut away from the ball. Any of the three can become an offense in itself. On the other hand, a team could use the basic cuts of all three tactics, putting in the plays which suits its personnel best. In that regard, a team can deploy its personnel into the slots where they will have the best chance of creating team success (e.g., making sure the jump shooters are moving out, while the big players are moving into the basket area).

A team will want to include the pinch-the-post, the screen and roll, the inside hand off, the outside hand off, back-door cuts, middle cuts, and the swing & go in its offense. The execution of all of these maneuvers is developed by two-on-two and three-on-three drills. Furthermore, a team might even want to run options from the wings, get the corners more involved, or even create more weakside movement. The next three chapters examine this theme.

Offense from the Wings

The ball is at the wing in almost all of the part plays that have been discussed to this point. It can be reversed easily from this angle because the weakside wing has run his Rules To Replace, supplanting 1 in the void at the point. It is also the perfect slope for entry into a posting player at either the low post, the middle post, or the high post. There are special plays, however, that can be run from the wing position.

The Screen Downs

Which screen down a team wishes to run depends on the talents of the player occupying the 2 spot. If the 2 player is a good jump shooter or a good one-on-one player, a team will generally want to run the option depicted in Diagram 6-1. If 2 is bigger, less mobile, but very strong around the basket, a team may opt for the scheme shown in Diagram 6-2.

In Diagram 6-1, 2 passes to 3 and screens down for 4. 1 is cutting away from the ball, while 3 and 5 are running the weakside Rules To Replace. 4, who is more of the inside type of player, breaks off of 2's screen. 4 then breaks on the high side of the screen like he is going outside for the jump shot. When 4 peels toward the goal, 2 breaks back off of 4's cut, using 4 as a cutting screen. This tactic gets a team's best player, 2, the ball nearer the basket.

If 4 is as good a jump shooter as 2, a team may then want to run the pattern suggested in Diagram 6-2. 3 and 5 again execute the weakside cuts called by the Rules

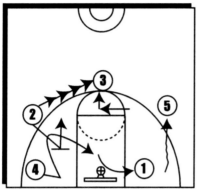

Diagram 6-1

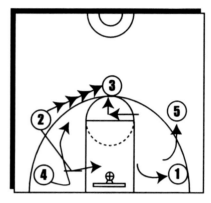

Diagram 6-2

To Replace. 1 is cutting away from the ball. 2 passes to 3 and screens down for 4. This time, 4 dips and breaks off of 2's screen for a pass and a possible jump shot. 2 rolls to the basket for a pass and a potential three point play. 3 reads X2. If a "switch" occurs, 2 is the primary receiver. If no switch is called, 4 is the primary receiver.

Weave With Stationary Screen

2 has the ball. 1 has cut away or basket cut. 1 can either be going to weakside to fill in for 5, who is filling in for 3, or be filling in for 4. 4 has run the side-post curl to the high post. 4 should be facing the basket. 2 passes back out to 3 (Diagram 6-3). 3 fakes to his left and dribbles toward 4's outside shoulder. 2 dips and comes off of 3's shoulder for a hand-off pass. 2 dribble drives around both 3 and the screening 4. 2 reads X4. If X4 stays with 4, 2 dribble drives to the basket. If X4 "switches," 4 cuts to the basket (rolls to basket if he is not already facing the basket) for a return pass from 2 and a lay-up.

Diagram 6-3

Pinch the Post From the Wing

Diagram 6-4 shows 1 cutting to fill 4's voided space. 4 runs the side-post curl, ending up near the high post. 2 passes the ball to 4 and runs the pinch-the-post maneuver with 4. a team Needs The Three-Point Shot

Diagram 6-4

Diagram 6-5

During the course of a season there are times that a team must have a three-point shot. A relatively easy way to get the three-point shot is illustrated in Diagram 6-5. In this example, a team's best three-point shooter, 2, has the ball. 4 runs the side-post curl. 3 is in the process of completing his weakside Rules To Replace. 2 passes to 3 and cuts very hard to the basket. 2 goes all the way to the basket because X2 must follow him or give the easy lay-up. This tactic also gives 4 an opportunity to set up the perfect angle. 2 comes back around 4's screen, racing hard to the three-point line. X4 has had to stay above 4 for fear 4 will post him up in the middle of the lane. X2 has also had to stay above 2 for the same reason. 4 then sets the screen on X2 which forces X2 to go over the top of the screen.

2's break to the three-point arc should be done in a manner that eliminates any possibility that X4 could get to him. 2 uses the stride stop, with the heals of his right foot hitting the floor just beyond the arc. 2 reverse pivots just as his balance is recovered by transferring his weight from heel to toe of his right foot. At this point, 2 has his shoulders squared to the basket, and 3 is delivering the pass at the letters of 2. 2 then catches the pass, turns, and lifts, extends, and flips the ball toward the basket.

Summary

A team's offense does not have to always begin from the point position. The offense can begin just as easily from the wing position. By beginning its offense from the point, all of a team's players should know which options are coming. As a consequence, they can react accordingly. After drilling extensively on the screen and roll, the pinch the post, the back-door cuts, etc., a team's offense can be executed from any angle. This diversity of options illustrates the beauty of the motion offense, especially when the post is open. Chapter 7 discusses how a team can bring the corners more into play.

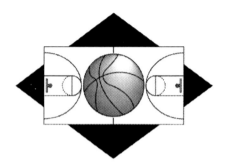

Getting the Corners More Involved

As a rule, we do not like to pass the ball into the corner, because too many bad things can occur. For example, the corner is the perfect place for the defense to trap; it provides the offense with the weakest angles to enter the ball into the post position; and it allows aggressive defenses tremendous weakside sagging opportunities.

The corner always has the option of running the side-post curl. This tactic can get him involved in many of the two- and three-player plays that have already been discussed. This chapter examines many of the quick-hitting ways that the strongside corner can get involved in the offense. In the next chapter, several of the ways to get the weakside corner, as well as the weakside wing; more involved are discussed.

Back-Door and Middle Cut

As 1 brings the ball down the floor, the corner player can be maneuvering his defender into possible mistakes. Should a defensive lapse occur, the corner needs to read it and take advantage of it immediately. In Diagram 7-1, 4 is walking toward the baseline. If X4 drifts more toward the baseline, 4 should plant his right foot, push hard, use the swim technique with his right arm, and break into the center of the lane. 4 should then have X4 on his back for the post-up position and a possible three-point play.

If 4 sees X4 playing a little too far up the lane toward the ball, he should walk X4 up toward the dribbling 1 (Diagram 7-2). At the point when 4 feels he has the

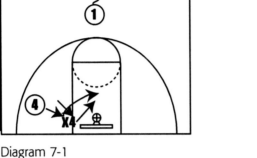

Diagram 7-1   Diagram 7-2

advantage, he should raise an open palm, signaling to 1 that he intends to break back door. 1 can then deliver the lob pass around the rim for a possible dunk or at least a power lay-up. 4 should never bring this pass back down below his chin, even if he has to return to the floor with the ball. 4 might even consider using pump fakes if his defender recovers sufficiently.

Exchange

Many teams have at least one very effective wing-denial defender. This talented denial defender can change the outcome of a game unless a team has a drilled strategy to combat such pressure. Faced with such asituation, the offense should exchange the wing for a corner player. In essence, this tactic takes that accomplished denial defender out of his game and provides the opposing team with a simpler entry into its offense.

In Diagram 7-3, 1 dribbles the ball down the floor. 2 is denied the ball by an skillful defender. 2 calls the exchange. To execute this exchange, 2 must make X2 follow him. This tactic is best accomplished by having 2 move directly toward the basket, never crossing paths with 4 or his defender. X2 must follow or give 2 the lay-up. 4 moves

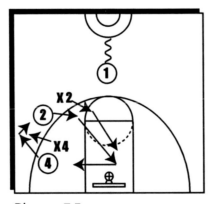

Diagram 7-3

more outside without taking a dip. On occasion, it is not that a player is an exceptionally talented denial defender as it is a difference in quickness. Whenever a team's perimeter player has a much quicker defender on him, the offensive team should allow him to exchange with the corner player. Just as a difference in size should send a team's attacker inside to take advantage of a contrast in player dimensions, a team should send any attacker whose defender is much quicker inside. As a consequence, the number of turnovers should shrink proportionally.

Screen Across With Roll

Diagram 7-4 illustrates 1 passing to 2 and cutting away from the ball. 4, who had already begun a cut inside, continues across the lane, calling 5's name. 5 breaks off of 4's screen. 4 then rolls back to the ball. 2 reads X4. If X4 "switches", 4 becomes the primary receiver. If no switch occurs, 5 should be open for the lay-up. A pass inside to either 4 or 5 can result in 4 and 5 playing the high-low inside game. If 4 receives the pass, he can check 5's position inside. If 5 gets the pass, 4 should cut down the lane in hope of either getting the middle cut or the lob pass over his defender on the back-door cut. Both areas are cleared out.

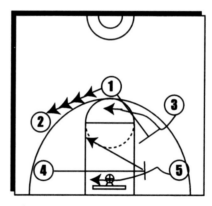

Diagram 7-4

This play is another great pattern to be used against zone defenses, the match-up, and half-court traps whether person-to-person or zone. A minor adjustment can be made to make it even more effective: For example, a team could let 5 step out to the short corner before going to replace 4's void. This short-corner position is an ideal location against zones, the match-up, and traps.

Corner To High-Post Screen

As 1 is bringing the ball down the floor, 4 begins to call his name and holds up his fist. 1 knows a back screen is going to occur. 1 then passes to 2, dips, and cuts off of 4's screen (Diagram 7-5). 1 replaces 4 in the corner, and 4 supplants 1.

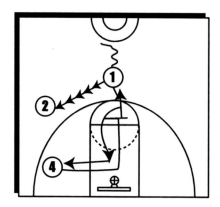

Diagram 7-5

Screen and Roll With Wing

In Diagram 7-6, 1 passes to 2 and cuts to the basket. 3 moves to the spot 1 vacated per the Rules To Replace. 5 supplants 3. 1 takes 5's old spot. In the meantime, 4 calls 2's name. 2 dribbles off of 4's screen. 4 rolls to the basket. If a switch occurs, 4 is open. If no switch happens, 2 should have the option of either the driving lay-up or, at the least, an unencumbered jump shot.

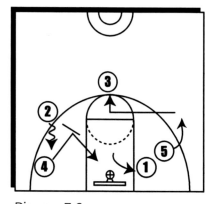

Diagram 7-6

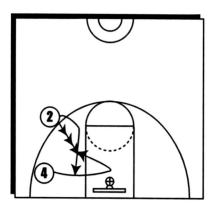

Diagram 7-7

Post Up or Pinch The Post

In Diagram 7-7 (similar to the situation shown in Diagram 7-6), 1 passes to 2 and cuts to the basket. 3, 5, and 1 have their defenders busy as they use their Rules to Replace. This procedure frees up 2 and 4 to play a two-player game. As 4 runs his side-post curl, he takes his defender deep into the lane before returning. 2 can either pass the ball inside to 4 for post-up moves or pass the ball inside to 4 and run the pinch-the-post game. In Diagram 7-7, 2 dips toward the center of the court and pinches the post while going to the outside of 4. 2 could just as easily dip toward the corner and pinch the post off of 4 while going to the center of the court. Both areas are adequately cleared out.

Swing and Go

As 1 brings the ball down the floor, 2 takes his defender into the second-lane block. At this point, 4 has taken his defender into the region near the basket (Diagram 7-8). As 1 approaches the top of the key, 4 swings around 2 in the old swing-and-go pattern. As a general rule, X2 aids in the completion of this part play. X2 will be above 2, trying to keep 2 from posting up. As 4 swings around 2, X4 must fight both 2's screen and X2's body. If a pass is completed to 4, X2 often has a habit of thinking he must help on the penetrating pass. At this instance, 2 rolls to the basket with his right hand up as a target. An easy jump shot by 4 or an uncontested lay-up by 2 often results.

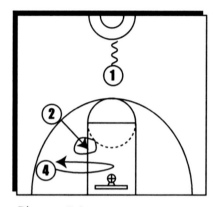

Diagram 7-8

Summary

Many creative ways exist to get the corner player involved in the offense without passing the ball into the corner. In this chapter, several of these ways for the strongside corner player were presented. In Chapter 10, methods of getting both the weakside wing and the weakside corner more involved in the offense will be discussed.

8

Weakside Involvement

Two basic movements from the weakside offer excellent scoring opportunities. The next section examines these opportunities in greater detail.

Basic WeakSide Movement

Diagram 8-1 illustrates the weakside-wings Rules to Replace the spot vacated by 1. It is the best part play to score against person-to-person defenses, as well as a strong method to reverse the ball against zone defenses. It also provides an outlet against teams that trap the first pass.

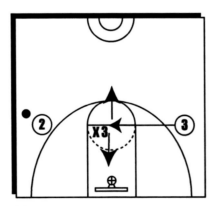

Diagram 8-1

2 has the ball. 1 has already cut to the basket. 3 is replacing 1's void. 2 and 3 both read the coverage offered by X3. If X3 is above the line between 2 and 3, 3 will back-door cut. If X3 is below the line between 2 and 3, 3 will pop out for the reversal pass. 5 replaces 3 spot (Diagram 8-1). If 3 cuts back door, 5 can now begin to replace 1's old spot, employing the same strategy with 2 as 3 had previously used. This tactic allows a continuity to develop that is ideal as a freeze or stall, as well as a scoring opportunity.

Diagrams 8-2 and 8-3 provide 5 with another option. Instead of filling for 3, who was replacing 1, 5 can observe how X5 is playing him as he moves up to supplant 3's void. If X5 is anticipating 5's movement up toward 3's old position, X5 might overplay the situation. When this occurs, 5 can cut back door for the pass from 2 and a lay-up (Diagram 8-2). On the other hand, after seeing 5 replace 3 several times, X5 might decide to sag excessively toward the basket because he knows that 5 is not making an attacking move. When this occurs, 5 can easily cut to the middle and get X5 on his back for a post-up maneuver (Diagram 8-3).

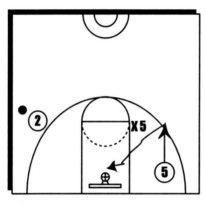

Diagram 8-2

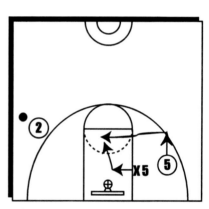

Diagram 8-3

Flash Pivot & Lob

The weakside corner should always read the cutting that is appearing in the lane. The weakside corner should never congest the area. At times, however, the area around the lane is wide open. For instance, if 1 cuts to the ball and 3 is running his Rules To Replace, the area around the basket and the lane is literally beckoning for a flash-pivot cut. This situation happens frequently during the course of a game.

Diagram 8-4 displays the flash pivot by 5. 2 and 5 read X5. If X5 trails 5, the pass can easily be made inside to 5. 5 has the entire weakside baseline open for a one-on-one move close to the basket. If X5 overplays 5 to prevent 5 from getting the inside pass, 5 raises his open palm toward 2. This signal is 2's key to toss the lob pass near the basket. 5 goes to get the pass, waiting until the ball has passed over the head of

X5. 5 should not bring this pass back down. Even if the pass was such that 5 must bring the ball back down, 5 should never bring it below his chin. Pump fakes are also an option should X5 recover well enough to defend the power lay-up.

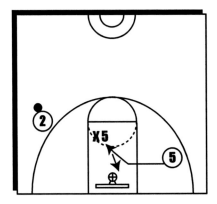

Diagram 8-4

Pinch The Post With 5

Preferably, the weakside corner should not get too involved inside the key. On the other hand, movement into the key area does compel X5 to play all 5's maneuvers honestly. Instead of overplaying 5's flash cut, X5 plays behind 5. 2 does not make the pass into the lane to 5 for a one-on-one move. 5 continues to the side-high post for a pass from 2 and a pinch-the-post tactic (Diagram 8-5).

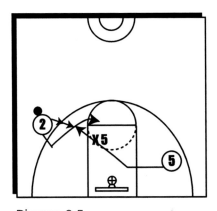

Diagram 8-5

Back-Door Lob To THE WeakSide Wing

If X5 is conscious of 5's inside maneuverability, the lob pass to the weakside wing becomes an excellent scoring play. In Diagram 8-6, 5 has read X5 and X3 correctly. X5 is going to deny any flash to the ball by 5, and X3 intends to pressure 3's Rules To

Replace movement. 5 calls 3's name and raises his fist. This action keys 3 that a backdoor cut is open. 2 should throw the semi-lob pass up around the rim for 3. Again, 3 should not bring this pass down. If circumstances require 3 returning to the floor with the ball, however, he should never bring it below chin level. Pump fakes are also an option as well.

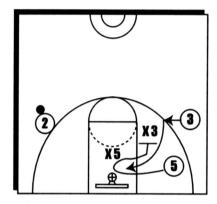

Diagram 8-6

An Effective Zone Variation

Many screening opportunities exist for the weakside corner player. One particularly effective option is illustrated in Diagram 8-7. In Diagram 8-7, both corner players get involved in screening. 1 should be a team's best outside shooter. This play is an excellent scoring opportunity against zone defenses. It also works very well as a last-second scoring play. 1 passes to 2 and then cuts to the basket. 3 runs his Rules To Replace technique. 2 holds the ball to see which corner screen 1 will use, the strongside or the weakside. In Diagram 8-7, 1 employs the weakside screen. 2 reverses the pass to 3, who then passes to 1 in the corner. After 5 has set his screen, 5 should reverse pivot for a post-up move. 1 has the option to shoot, to fake a shot and drive if his defender races out to cover him, or to dump the pass inside to the posting 5.

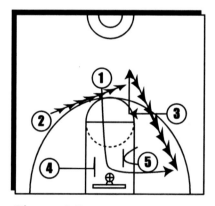

Diagram 8-7

Summary

In previous chapters, the three basic movements—cut to the basket, cut to the ball, and cut away from the ball—have been discussed in detail. Several ideas about establishing an offense before cutting begins have also received elaboration. Furthermore, additional options for the weakside, offenses from the wings, and getting the corners more involved have been reviewed. The key point to keep in mind, however, is that a team should not allow its offense to get too complicated. All factors considered, a coach should adhere to one coherent philosophical guidepost: Stay simple. Don't choose them all. Choose the ones which are best suited to your team's personnel for this particular year. A number of play patterns have also been examined as parts of a zone offense, as segments to be used as a stall, as components against half court trapping, and as part plays for a last-shot opportunity. In other words, the Five Player Open Post can be developed into a multiple offense.

Knowing the patterns and movements a team wants its players to learn is not enough, however. Each player should know how to execute those part plays without ruining the freedom of choice that is available in the Five Player Open Post Motion Offense. Experience strongly suggests that extensive drilling is the best way for players to learn their roles and responsibilities. In the next two chapters (9 and 10), many of the drills a team should use to teach its players the part plays of the offense are presented.

9

Individual & Two-on-Two Drills

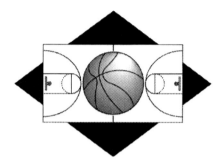

Drilling has been shown to be one of the best ways for coaches to determine if their players can execute a particular technique or fundamental properly. Because many drills tend to involve less than 5-on-5 situations, a coach can focus his concentration on fewer individuals. The individual attention given to players can allow them to develop their skills more quickly. Furthermore, when drilling, players must *concentrate* more deeply and play with more *intensity*—two of the primary ingredients of successful performance.

Drilling also teaches the offense in part style under highly competitive conditions. A team should initially teach the whole part, then break down into drilling that particular part, and then return to teaching the whole part. This approach enables its players to better understand what is expected of them.

Drilling should be made both competitive and fun. Drilling should also adhere to a basic structure that is easily followed without having to learn a new set of rules for each drill. For example, players always rotate from offense to defense to the end of the line. That format is very easy to remember. No matter what the drill, players go from offense to defense to the end of line.

Every player should learn every position. Accordingly, every player should drill at every position. Each drill should be moved to other areas of the court from time to time: One day, a player should drill on the right side of the court, the next day on the left side. As many angles as possible should be practiced. While some decrement will typically occur from a player's performance in a drill and subsequently in a game, these lapses tend to reduce as the season progresses. As a general rule, most players improve their game performance over the course of a season.

While drilling, a team should be practicing against its next opponent. If its next opponent plays in the passing lanes, that's how it should drill. If the opponent sags, the team should work on its offense against the sag. If the opponent double teams the first pass or the first dribble, a team's drills for that week should stress working against that defensive tactic.

In this chapter, individual and two-player drills are presented. The next chapter brings a third attacker and a third defender into the foray.

Individual Cutting Drills

The Five Player Open Post Motion Offense includes the middle cut, the back-door cut, and post-up mechanisms. The basic six movements are covered from all the angles in this chapter. All of these individual drills can be made into two-on-two drills by merely placing a defender on 2.

Point Cuts

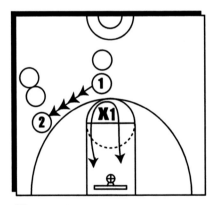

Diagram 9-1

- Line players up as shown in Diagram 9-1.

- Players rotate from 1 to X1 to the end of 2's line; 2 rotates to the end of 1's line.

- 1 passes to 2 and reads X1 defense. A good defender will jump to the ball. In that case, 1 back doors X1. In rare cases, X1 will drop too deeply into the lane. When that occurs, 1 can middle cut. In no case should 1 cut close to the ball. If the defense intends to double team, the defense should be made to go a great distance. Using either the middle or the back-door cut, 1 goes all the way to the basket. Now 1 either can make a decision to follow the Rules To Replace or can, if X1 allows it, come back toward 2 for a post up.

- Begin the drill by requiring X1 to play dummy defense. Tell X1 how he should play (i.e., jump to the ball, slide to the basket, go double team 2, allow the post-up move). Then, permit X1 to play defense, making his own judgments.the defense intends to double team, the defense should be made to go a great distance. Using either the middle or the back-door cut, 1 goes all the way to the basket. Now 1 either can make a decision to follow the Rules To Replace or can, if X1 allows it, come back toward 2 for a post up.

Objectives:

- To teach the back-door or middle cut.
- To teach posting up.
- To teach Rules to Replace.

5's Rules To Replace Cut

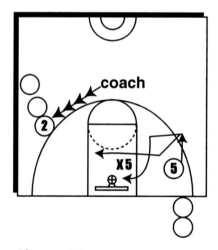

Diagram 9-2

Procedures:

- Line players up as shown in Diagram 9-2.
- Rotate from 5 to X5 to the end of 2's line; 2 rotates to the end of 5's line.
- Conduct the drill as follows: 5 replaces the void left by 3, per Rules To Replace. As 5 moves to replace 3's spot, 5 watches X5. If an opportunity exists to cut because of X5's mistake, 5 reads and cuts. 5 can either continue to post up or go back to the corner per Rules to Replace.

Objectives:

- To teach 5 proper movement in Rules to Replace.
- To teach the back-door and middle cuts.
- To teach posting up.

3's Rules To Replace Cuts

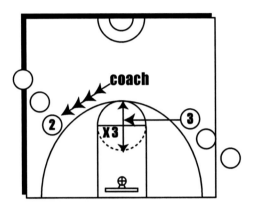

Diagram 9-3

Procedures:

- Line players up as shown in Diagram 9-3.
- Rotate from 3 to X3 to the end of line 2; 2 rotates to the end of 3's line.
- Conduct the drill as follows: 3 makes his Rules To Replace cut. 3 has the option of either going back door or middle cutting or popping out to replace 1's void. 3 also has a choice to continue his cut across the free-throw line and run a pinch-the-post tactic with 2. Should 3 cut back door, he cuts to the basket. If his defender plays him wrong at that juncture, 3 can reverse pivot and post up.

Objectives:

- To teach Rules to Replace.
- To teach back-door or middle cut.
- To teach proper pop-out techniques.
- To teach pinch-the-post tactics.
- To teach posting-up maneuvers.

Corner's Original Cut

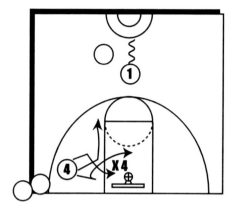

Diagram 9-4

Procedures:

- Line players up as shown in Diagram 9-4.

- Rotate from 4 to X4 to the end of line 1; 1 rotates to the end of line 4.

- Conduct the drill as follows: 4 can run a back-door or a middle cut as 1 is bringing the ball up the court. 4 must read X4 to be successful. 4 can run the side-post curl pattern to receive a pass at side-high post from 1. If the team is drilling for individual cuts, 4 should go one on one against X4. If the team is running two-on-two, 1 and 4 can run the pinch-the-post tactic.

Objectives:

- To teach the back-door lob or the middle cut for posting up.

- To teach side-post curl pattern.

- To teach Rules to Replace.

- To teach pinch-the-post maneuvers.

Wing Back-Door or Middle Cut

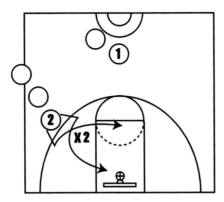

Diagram 9-5

Procedures:

- Line players up as in Diagram 9-5.

- Rotate from 2 to X2 to the end of line 1; 1 rotates to the end of line 2.

- Conduct the drill as follows: As 1 is bringing the ball down the floor, 2 has the option of using a back-door or a middle cut. 4, not shown, rotates up to fill 2's vacated void. 2 then applies Rules to Replace by cutting into the corner where 4 was originally.

- This drill could be varied as follows: 2 could start with ball and pass to 1. Upon completing this pass to 1, 2 chooses to make one of his cuts.

Objectives:

- To teach the wing to back-door or middle cut.

- To teach the wing to make a pass to reverse the ball (variation).

- To teach the wing his Rules To Replace.

Many other individual cuts exist. Any cutting movement inside this offense can be made into an individual cutting drill. Even better, the wide-open Five Player Open Post Motion Offense can be expanded by adding a coach's favorite cut to it. That feature is another beauty of this offensive system.

Two-on-Two Drills

When a coach initially starts to build his team's offense by part plays, he should first teach the entire team offense, then begin to add instructional drills, starting with one-on-one individual movement. The next step is to incorporate two-on-two maneuvers into the drilling schedule.

Screen & Roll on the Ball

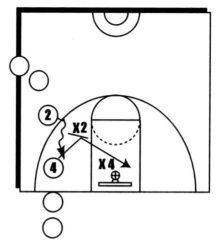

Diagram 9-6

Procedures:

- Line players up as shown in Diagram 9-6

- Rotate from 2 to X2 to the end of 4's line; rotate from 4 to X4 to the end of 2's line.

- Conduct the drill as follows: Run the drill between the point and the wing—between the weakside 3 (when 3 comes to replace 1), and 2 and between the side post curling 4 and 2 or 4 and 1. The drill should be performed at different spots on the court every other day or so. To successfully execute the screen and roll, 2 must step away from 4, using rocker step moves. 2 knows 4 is coming to set the screen because 4 is calling 2's name, and 4 has his fist up. Because 4 knows 2 is going to set up X2 for the screen, 4 sets the screen on the high side of X2's body. This makes tough fpr X2 to slide through. 4 reverse pivots and pins X2 on his back. At this point, a switch must occur or 2 will drive for the lay-up. If a switch happens, X2 will be on 4's back. 4 then rolls to the basket for a pass back from 2 and the lay-up. To perform this tactic correctly, 4 rolls to the basket in a parallel drive to 2's dribbling drive.

Objectives:

- To teach correct screening techniques.

- To teach players how to set up their defender for the screen.

- To teach precise screen and roll mechanics.

- To teach Rules to Replace.

Inside Hand Offs

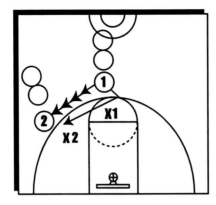

Diagram 9-7

Procedures:

- Line players up as shown in Diagram 9-7.

- Rotate from 1 to X1 to the end of line 2; rotate 2 to X2 to the end of line 1.

- Conduct the drill as follows: Begin the drill by impelling X2 to drop off of 2. This read is the one that activates the inside hand off as part of the Five Player Open Post Motion Offense. 1 passes to 2 and dips.

- 1 cuts inside 2. 1 has in effect set a screen for 2 to shoot over if he does not hand off to 1. This is the first option. The second choice is for 1 to set the screen on X2. At this point, both players must read. If a "switch" occurs, the screen and roll takes place with a return pass to 1 being the best option. If there is a call for "switch" too early, 1 "splits the switch" by planting his outside foot and cutting hard to basket for a pass from 2. If 2 hands off to 1, 2 should do so by holding the ball on his left hip and placing the ball into 1's hands as he cuts by. 1 immediately begins a drive to the basket. Usually X1 will follow. If, for any reason, X2 feels he has to stop 1's drive as well, thereby putting two defenders on 1, 2 should find the open spot for the return pass and easy shot. Often, 1 will drive X1 into X2 because of X2's sag.

Objectives:

- To teach how to hand-off on inside screens.

- To teach "split-the-screen" techniques.

- To teach the screen and roll.

- To teach shooting over a screen.

- To teach attacking sagging defenders; to teach Rules to Replace.

Outside Hand Offs

Diagram 9-8

Procedures:

• Line players up as shown in Diagram 9-8.

• Rotate from 1 to X1 to the end of line 2; rotate from 2 to X2 to the end of line 1.

• 1 passes to 2, dips, and cuts outside 2. At this point, 1 and 2 read X1. If X1 tries to fight over the top, 2 reverse pivots, like in the pinch-the-post maneuvers. If no switch occurs, 2 hands off to 1 who drives to the basket. 2 then rolls for the rebound or a pass back. If X2 opens up to let X1 slide through, 1 has the three-point shot over a screen. 1 can use 2 after the hand off. 1 can let 2 read where X1 is. 2 sets a screen on X1, and 1 reads the side on which the screen is set. 1 drives off this screen. 1 and 2 then execute the screen and roll.

• If there is an early "switch" call, 2 can "split the switch".

Objectives:

• To teach outside hand offs.

• To teach the screen and roll.

• To teach shooting over a screen.

• To teach footwork of the pinch-the-post tactic.

• To teach "split-the-switch" techniques.

Pinch The Post

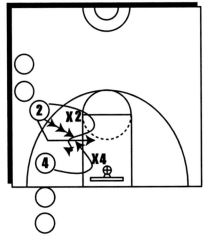

Diagram 9-9

Procedures:

- Line players up as shown in Diagram 9-9.

- Rotate from 2 to X2 to the end of line 4; rotate from 4 to X4 to the end of line 2.

- Conduct the drill as follows: 4 runs the side-post curl pattern. 2 passes the ball inside to 4. 2 has the choice of running the pinch the post across the middle of the court or along the baseline side. To successfully execute the pinch the post, the proper foot work must be mastered. For example, 2 dips to the baseline side, then cuts across the middle. 2 should run directly at 4's body. Just as 2 gets to 4, 4 reverse pivots on his left foot. 2 cuts off of 4's left shoulder, rubbing X2 off onto 4's back. If no switch occurs, 4 hands off to 2 who can either drive all the way to the basket or pull up for the short jump shot. If a switch happens, 4 puts the ball out on his left side for one dribble and a slam dunk or lay-up. X2 is on 4's back and cannot stop the lay-up. The pinch-the-post should be run from all the angles that are available from this offense (i.e., one day from the wing and corner; the next day, from two other positions).

Objectives:

- To teach the dip to set up the pinch the post.

- To teach the footwork of the pinch the post.

- To teach Rules to Replace.

- To teach the side-post curl pattern.

Swing & Go

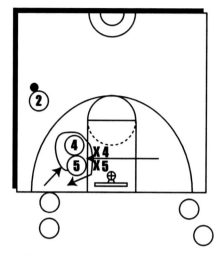

Diagram 9-10

Procedures:

- Line players up as shown in Diagram 9-10.

- Rotate from 4 to X4 to the end of 5's line; rotate from 5 to X5 to the end of 2's line; rotate from 2 to the end of 4's line.

- Conduct the drill as follows: 2 begins with the ball. 5 cuts along the baseline; and 4 cuts into thebig block area. 5 runs the swing and go around 4. If X5 follows 5, X4 front pivots into X5. 5 should have the jump shot. If X4 switches off onto 5, 4 rolls to basket with right hand up as target for a pass. 4 should then have X5 on his back. If X5 tries to sag around X4 to wait for 5 to come around the swing and go, 5 steps out for the short jumper. If X4 switches, 5 stops short of coming around the swing for the short jumper. Often, X4 and X5 will be in doubt as to their coverage. As a result, they frequently run into each other, trying to get the correct coverage.

Objectives:

- To teach the swing-and-go pattern.

- To teach the swing-and-go inside passing.

- To teach the wing how to read the defensive coverage on 4 and 5, so that he'll know exactly when to pass the ball inside.

Summary

At this point in the book, almost the entire system of the Five Player Open Post Motion Offense has been presented. Chapter 9 covered drills to develop the individual movements, as well as the two-on-two part plays of the offense. The three-on-three offensive part plays are discussed in the next chapter.

10

Three-On-Three Drills

There are many places in the Five Player Open Post Motion Offense where three players can develop a three-player game. At any of those spots, a three-on-three drill can be created. This chapter presents five of those options. Similar to the individual and 2-on-2 drills, 3-on-3 drills should be conducted on one side of the court one day and on the other side the next day. The numbered personnel involved should be changed periodically.

Screen Away & Roll

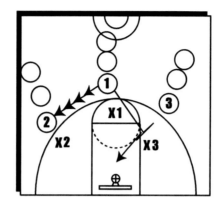

Diagram 10-1

Procedures:

- Line players up as shown in Diagram 10-1.

- Rotate from 1 to X1 to the end of line 2; rotate from 2 to X2 to the end of line 3; rotate from 3 to X3 to the end of line 1.

- Conduct the drill as follows: 1 can begin the drill by passing to either side. 2 and 3 can, if they are being overplayed, middle cut or back-door cut (or at least dip to replace themselves). 1 has option of going and screening away, as depicted in Diagram 10-1, or cutting to the basket and then setting the back screen. 1 goes to screen away. 3 dips to set up his defender. 1 calls 3's name and raises his fist. 1 sets the screen on the high side of X3, compelling X3 to go beneath the screen. As X3 attempts to go below the screen, 1 reverse pivots (putting X3 on his back) and rolls to the basket. This option is best when 3 is the better jump shooter and 1 is the bigger player. This tactic typically results in a substantial mismatch both outside and inside. 2 reads X1. If a switch occurs, the screener, 1, becomes the primary receiver, while 3 becomes the secondary receiver. If no switch happens, 3 is the primary receiver, and 1 becomes the secondary receiver. If the switch is called too early, 1 splits the switch and goes hard to the basket. 4 and 5 could be added to the drill without defenders and teach the Rules to Replace.

Objectives:

- To teach the screen and roll away from the ball; to teach 2 to read the screen and roll for the primary receiver; to teach screening from different angles; to teach dips in setting up screens; to teach the back-door and middle cuts; to teach Rules to Replace.

Split The Post

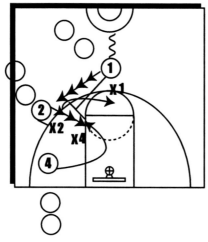

Diagram 10-2

Procedures:

- Line players up as shown in Diagram 10-2.

- Rotate from 1 to X1 to the end of line 2; rotate from 2 to X2 to the end of line 4; rotate from 4 to X4 to the end of line 1.

- Conduct the drill as follows: As 1 brings the ball down the floor, 4 runs the side-post curl. 1 has option of passing to the cutting 4 or to 2, who then feeds 4. 2 can cut back door, allowing 4 to run Rules to Replace, with 2 and 4 exchanging places and responsibilities. In Diagram 10-2, 1 passes to 2 and calls out 2's name. 1 raises his fist. 2 passes to 4. At this point, 1 and 4 have set a double screen for 2. It should be noted that the tactic could have just as easily involved a staggered screen.

- Once 2 dips and cuts off of the double screen, 1 races around 4 for a cut to the basket, activating the pinch-the-post series. Depending on how X1 defenses the play, 1 does not have to go around 4. If X1 did not switch, 2 has the hand off. As a result 1 should go around 4 for a possible pass back from 2 or to act as a rebounder on 2's shot. If X1 switched, then X2 is on the side away from 2 with the responsibility of covering 1. Accordingly, 1 should roll back in the same direction as 2. 4 should then reverse pivot or front pivot into X2's path and run the pinch the post.

Objectives:

- To teach the back-door and middle cut; to teach the side-post curl pattern.

- To teach setting a proper double screen (or a staggered screen); to teach pinch-the-post maneuvers; to teach Rules to Replace, especially if 3 and 5 are added to the drill without defenders; to teach proper ball handling in relatively tight situations.

Dribble Weave Into Post Screen

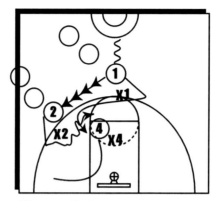

Diagram 10-3

Procedures:

- Line players up as shown in Diagram 10-3.

- Rotate from 1 to X1 to the end of line 2; rotate from 2 to X2 to the end of line 4; rotate from 4 to X4 to the end of line 1.

- Conduct the drill as follows: 1 has the option of performing a dribbling weave or passing to 2 and letting him begin the weave. In Diagram 10-3, 1 passes to 2. 2 then begins his dribble toward 4, who has finished his side-post curl pattern. 2 is calling out 1's name. 1 dips and races off 2's screen. 2 has the option of keeping his dribbling weave going. 2 reads X1's coverage. If X1 does not switch, 2 keeps the ball. If X1 switches, 2 hands off to 1. At this point, 1 has the choice of either continuing around 4's screen or 1 rubbing off X2 onto 4. 1 can accomplish this by dribbling back in the direction of 2.

Objectives:

- To teach the dribbling weave with a post screener.

- To teach 4 to screen for the dribblers.

- To teach 4 to run the side-post curl pattern.

- To teach Rules to Replace, especially if 3 and 5 are added to the drill without defenders.

Staggered Screens

A number of ways exist in which to set a staggered screen. The one exhibited in Diagram 10-4 makes use of a dribbler off of the screens. Situations in the offense exist, however, where the staggered screen can be set for a screener away from the ball. At those places in the offense, a drill should be employed to make it a part play of the offense.

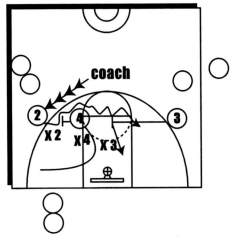

Diagram 10-4

Procedures:

- Line players up as shown in Diagram 10-4.

- Rotate from 2 to X2 to end of line 3; rotate from 3 to X3 to end of line 4; rotate from 4 to X4 to end of line 2.

- Conduct the drill as follows: The coach passes to 2, while 4 is running the side-post curl. Meanwhile, 3 is following his Rules to Replace. Both 3 and 4 call out 2's name and set the staggered screen. If either X4 or X3 call out a switch, then their assignments — 3 and 4 respectively — roll to the basket. If everyone is covered properly, 3 has the option to post up at the very end of the play.

Objectives:

- To teach the staggered screen.

- To teach 2 to dribble off the shoulder of the screeners.

- To teach the screen on the ball and roll.

- To teach posting up techniques.

- To teach Rules to Replace, especially if 1 and 5 are added to the drill without defenders. In such a situation, 1 has the choice of replacing either the strongside corner or the weakside corner.

Flash Pivot & UCLA Pin

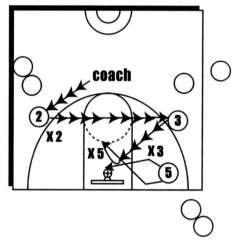

Diagram 10-5

Procedures:

- Line players up as shown in Diagram 10-5.

- Rotate from 2 to X2 to the end of line 3; rotate from 3 to X3 to the end of line 5; rotate from 5 to X5 to the end of line 2.

- Conduct the drill as follows: The coach passes to 2 and replaces himself (i.e., if 1 is added to the drill without a defender, 1 would replace himself). 5 flashes to the ball. 3 replaces himself. The first option available is for a pass inside to 5 for the one-on-one move against X5. 5 reads X5's coverage and tries to get his body between 2 and X5. If X5 overplays the pass, 2 throws the lob pass to 5. 5 seals X5, much as he would should he be on the big block and X5 were fronting him. 5 shows 2 his open palm, while he turns sideways to his defender. 5 puts his arm, bent at a 90-degree angle, into the back of X5. 5 holds this position until the lob pass is directly over his head. 5 then moves to receive the pass and a slam dunk or a power lay-up.

- Should none of these options be available, X5 must have a slight overplay. X3 must be sagging and helping on the lob pass. As a result, 2 passes to 3. 5 seals X5 on his back by reverse pivoting (this tactic is the old pinning move made famous by the great UCLA teams under renowned coach John Wooden). 3 immediately dumps the pass inside to 5 for the power lay-up. If X5 did not overplay, 2 can pass inside to 5 and run the pinch-the-post tactic.

Objectives:

- To teach the flash pivot.
- To teach posting up and sealing.
- To teach pinning maneuvers.
- To teach pinch the post.
- To teach lob passing.
- To teach Rules to Replace, especially if 1 and 4 are added to the drill without defenders.
- A number of variations of this drill are available for the astute and creative coach. For example, in Diagram 10-5, 1 could be added without a defender and 4 with a defender. This variation would allow 1 to pass to either side of the court and activate the drill from either side of the court. Variations of these types of drills are possible throughout the entire spectrum of the Five Player Open Post Motion Offense. In reality, these variations are too numerous for all of the possibilities to be presented in this book.

Summary

At this point in the text, the entire offense has been presented in full plan. Furthermore, the offense has been broken down into teaching drills, involving a single individual, two players, and three players. These drills can be used as shooting drills, as well as competitive drills. Perhaps most importantly, the players are learning the offense while they drill. The next three chapters cover four-player and five-player strategies..

11

Weakside and Other Drills

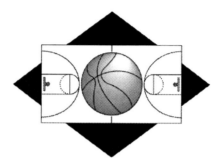

For a team to achieve the continuity and the functioning essential to maximal game performance, it must eventually drill with a full team of five attackers and five defenders. All players do not have to be active on every drill. For example, a coach can declare only the strongside players defense in a particular sequence; only the weakside defenders are alive in the next drill, etc. Such a tactic would permit the team to drill five attackers versus three defenders. Furthermore, those defenders who are actively participating in the drill could change as the ball changes sides of the court. This chapter presents five attackers against five defenders, with only a certain number of defenders playing live defense. This approach allows a team's players to learn their offense without always facing overly aggressive defense.

All of the offenses in this chapter begin from the standard formation. Initially, the only live defenders in the drill are the defenders X1, X2, and X3. After that, the play determines which of the defenders play live defense. Five-on-five play is discussed in the last two chapters of this book.

Full Play WeakSide Drill

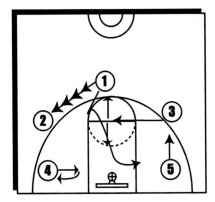

Diagram 11-1

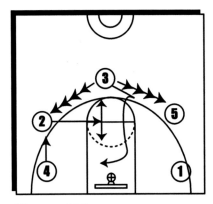

Diagram 11-2

Procedures:

- Line up players five-against-five in a regular Five Player Open Post Motion offensive formation.

- Rotate players from offense to defense to offense after a certain numbers of scores. (e.g., three).

- Keep in mind that while defenders will not be pictured in the diagrams, as in all sections of this book, X1 will guard 1, X2 on 2, X3 on 3, etc.

- Only three live defenders will be employed at a time during the entire play. Initially, those three defenders are X1, X2, and X3. These particular three defenders are attempting to deny the entry pass. Should one of those wing attackers attempt a back-door or a middle cut, the new wing replacement (Rules to Replace) defender will be live. For example, if 4 runs the side-post curl as 2 back doors his defender, then 4 replaces 2's void (per Rules To Replace), and X4 becomes a live defender.

- Once the pass goes into the wing, only the weakside defenders become live. In Diagram 11-1, the ball is entered to 2. As a result, the weakside becomes 3, 5, and 1. Accordingly, X3, X5, and X1 are live defenders. Once the pass is made back outside to 3, then X3, X2, and X5 are the live defenders.

- Diagram 11-2 illustrates the ball being reversed from Diagram 11-1. 2 passes to 3 who reverses the ball to 5 (Diagram 11-2). At this point, X3, X2 and X4 are the weakside defenders, and they play live defense.

Objectives:

- To teach the pattern for all five attackers.

- To teach attackers and defenders how to play from the weakside.

- To teach the entry pass into the wings (use the side-post curl and back-door cut, as well as 2 cutting back door and 4 just filling per Rules To Replace).

- To teach all players the Rules to Replace.

- To teach the weakside offense while the offensive players are under defensive pressure.

Screen Away Into Pinch The Post

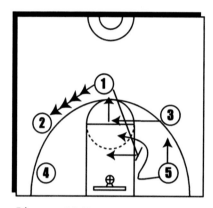

Diagram 11-3

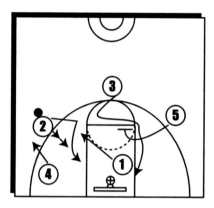

Diagram 11-4

Procedures:

- Conduct the drill as follows: In Diagram 11-3, 1 passes to 2 and goes to screen away for 5. 3 begins his Rules to Replace sequence. 5 comes off of 1's screen, but sees he is not open. 5 then moves out to replace 3's void (Rules to Replace). 1 rolls back to the basket, but 2 fails to get him the ball. 2 misread X1, otherwise 1 or 5 would have been open.

- At this point, the play goes from Diagram 11-3 to Diagram 11-4. The pattern does not stop. It continues. As a general rule, the pattern should never continue in the same manner in two successive attempts. That's the freedom given to a team's players in a motion offense. The players read and react. 1 pops up to the side post, where he receives a pass from 2. Meanwhile, 5 sets a back screen for 3. 3 hears 5 calling his name and sees 5's fist raised into the air. 3 then dips and cuts back door, using the screen. 1 checks for the bounce pass to 3 for the score. Meanwhile, 2 has begun running the pinch-the-post maneuver. 4 replaces 2's vacated spot.

- If no scoring opportunity exists, 5 has popped to the point. 3 has gone to the basket and cut back outside to his original position. 2 has cut into the corner where 5 started; 4 has filled 2's void; and 1, after passing to 5 at the point, should replace 4. At that point, the offense should continue.

- To place an even stronger emphasis on player and ball movement, a coach can require that only lay-ups count. Furthermore, the coach could insist that no consecutive movements by the offense can be the same. This procedure means that the offense must reverse the ball over and over until a lay-up results. This approach teaches the offense in its many forms to a team's players. Following this progression from Diagrams 11-3 and 11-4, the offense could not run the pinch the post again until some other maneuver, like the screen-and-roll or staggered screens, was run.

Objectives:

- To teach the pattern for all five attackers.

- To teach attackers and defenders how to play from the weakside.

- To teach the entry pass into the wings (use the side-post curl and the back-door cut, as well as 2 cutting back door and 4 just filling per Rules to Replace, if needed).

- To teach all players the Rules to Replace.

- To teach the weakside offense while the offensive players are under defensive pressure.

- To teach the players the need to make the offense continuous, and to always read their defenders and take advantage of what is offered.

WeaKSide Back Door Into StrongSide Double Screen

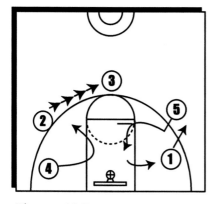

Diagram 11-5

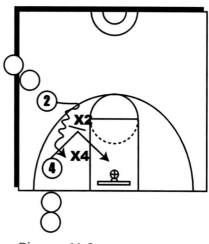

Diagram 11-6

This drill is designed to illustrate how a team's players can begin a weakside attack and, after one pass, turn it into a strongside attack.

Procedures:

- In Diagram 11-5, 1 passes to 2 and cuts to the basket. 3 follows his Rules To Replace and takes the point. 5 fills the void left by 3, per Rules To Replace. 1 fills the corner spot vacated by 5. The ball is reversed to 3. As the ball is being reversed to 3, 5 sees X5 dropping to the basket area. 5 takes advantage of this action by X5 by using a middle cut. 1 moves out to replace 5.

- 3 does not read 5's middle cut, but instead reverses the ball to 2 (Diagram 11-6). 5 moves out into the corner, per Rules To Replace. Meanwhile, 2 passes to 4 and calls 3's name. 2 and 4 set a double screen (or a staggered screen) for 3. They also activate the pinch-the-post series or the split-the-post sequence. 1 then begins his move to replace 3, per Rules To Replace.

Objectives:

- To teach the pattern for all five attackers.

- To teach attackers and defenders how to play from the weakside into the strongside continuity.

- To teach the entry pass into the wings (use the side-post curl and back-door cut, as well as 2 cutting back door and 4 just filling per Rules to Replace, if needed).

- To teach all players Rules to Replace.

- To teach the strongside offense while the offensive players are under defensive pressure.

- To teach the players the need to make the offense continuous, and to always read their defenders and take advantage of what is offered.

- To teach weakside movement in order to keep the defense from sagging and helping.

WeakSide Movement To Keep Defenders Busy

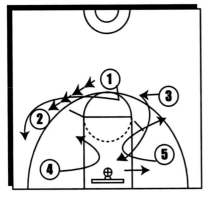

Diagram 11-7

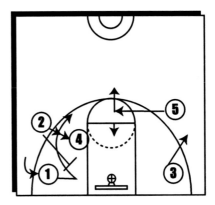

Diagram 11-8

One of the two least desirable things that can happen in a motion offense is for the weakside attackers to just stand around (or really even to replace themselves). The second least desirable thing for weakside attackers to do is make non-attacking movements. Diagrams 11-7 and 11-8 demonstrate how the weakside can have meaningful movement and keep their defenders occupied, while the offensive attack is concentrated on the other side of the court.

Procedures:

• In Diagram 11-7, 1 passes to 2 and cuts outside 2. 4 runs his side-post curl pattern. This tactic is 3's cue to break across the lane toward 2, who is running his Rules to Replace. 3, however, hears 5 calling his name and sees 5's raised fist. 5 is setting a back screen for 3. 3 cuts to the basket for the pass and the lay-up, if it is available. Meanwhile, 5 replaces 3's void.

• While the weakside movement did not produce a score, it did generate a meaningful attempt to score. Meanwhile, in Diagram 11-8, 2 passes to 4 and begins to call 1's name. 1 hears this call by 2 and sees 2's raised fist. The question arises at this particular point in the play: Is the weakside busy with intelligent movement? Yes. 5 is running his Rules to Replace, either going to the point or, if he is covered incorrectly, going for the back-door lay-up. 3 is cutting outside to fill for 5, but is also watching X3 for a chance to middle cut or back-door cut. The strongside is activating the split the post off of a staggered screen.

Objectives:

- To teach the pattern for all five attackers.

- To teach attackers and defenders how to play from the weakside into strongside continuity.

- To teach entry pass into the wings (use side post curl & back door, as well as 2 cutting back door and 4 just filling per Rules to Replace, if needed).

- To teach all players the Rules to Replace.

- To teach the strongside offense while it's under defensive pressure.

- To teach the players the need to make the offense continuous, and to always read their defenders and take advantage of what is offered.

- To teach weakside movement in order to keep the defense from sagging a n d helping.

Summary

At this point in the text, the offense can be seen in a team's full view. Information on how to create drills from part plays inside the offense has been presented. An explanation of how to generate continuous movement for a team's attackers has been covered. A discussion of how to keep the weakside defenders busy while the attack is happening on the strongside has also been reviewed. The only two critical areas that are left to be addressed are how to make the Five Player Open Offense multiple and how to drill the offense in such a way to teach the strategies of the offense being multiple. The final two chapters (12 and 13 respectively) examine these two issues.

12

Five Player Open Post as a Multiple Offense

As a general premise, eight basic types of offensive strategy exist in basketball. First, there is the strategy for dealing with the person-to-person defense. The Five Player Open Post Motion Offense was developed to defeat the person-to-person defense. This entire book could be used to attack that defense.

The other seven have specific sections in this chapter devoted to them: *delay, stall, zone, combinations, traps, the match-up*, and *the last-second shot*. If a single offensive attack can be used to manipulate each of those strategies, a coach should think of the practice time that could be saved teaching only one offense. Furthermore, a coach should think of how much simpler his job as an offensive coach would be. The Five Player Open Post Motion Offense works well in each of the aforementioned strategies. Some portions of the offense work better against particular types of defenses. When discussing that selective strategy, the portions that work best are pointed out. The basic offense against each defense is presented, and reference is made to the diagrams already presented in this book.

Diagram 1-7 shows the basic movement. Diagrams 11-1 and 11-2 present the change of sides as the ball is reversed from one side of the court to the other. When combined with Diagram 1-5, the side-post curl cut by the strongside corner, a team has the entire standard attack. These should be taught first, understood thoroughly, and then applied to the different defenses.

Delay

There are at least two times that a team should consider using *delay* tactics. The first instance in which it should be used is the last thirty seconds of each quarter to get the last shot of that quarter. That tactic will give a team four more meaningful possessions than its opponent. A lot of games are won by fewer than five points. Four more important possessions can provide a team with a significant point advantage. A team gains a meaningful possession by holding the ball and trying to score in the last 12 seconds. Its attempt to score usually ends with from three to five seconds left on the clock. A team's opponents race to throw the ball in and rush down the floor to try to score with a hurried shot. It's lucky if they hit the rim with the ball, let alone score. You got the last important possession in the quarter. The point that should be emphasized is that a team should run the <u>change of sides</u> until the last 12 seconds and then begin a pattern that was pre-arranged and pre-practiced. It does not matter who is at the point, who is at 2, or 3, etc. A team should be set to begin the pattern on a signal without having to reset.

The second time a team wants to use the delay is in the fourth quarter when the situation reaches a point where there are four minutes and the offensive team has at least a 12-point lead. A team should continue this strategy as long as three times the number of minutes is equal to or more than its lead. A team should run the delay, acting as though it intends to score, even if it is really just trying to run minutes off of the clock. Often, such a strategy will result in an uncontested lay-up.

The advantages of a delay are easily seen. For example, a team has a 7-point lead with two minutes left. The team is in its delay, and it manages to get one minute off of the clock before the other team fouls them. The offense then has free throws coming, up by seven points with only one minute left. In other words, barring a complete catastrophe, it's won. Great strategy. When running the *delay*, a team wants its players to remain aggressively attacking the basket and to look to score if possible.

To teach the *delay* as well as the *stall*, a team should use such maneuvers as those shown in Diagram 3-6. A team should make use of the drills that are illustrated in Diagrams 9-1, 9-2, and 9-3. The natural spread of the offense aids in both a team's *delay* and *stall* attack. A team doesn't want its players to spread further when running the *delay*, but it does want them to widen their positions when employing the *stall*.

Stall

The *stall* is different than the *delay*. A team is running its offense and trying to score in the delay—a lay-up, hopefully, but still an attempt to score. In the *stall*, a team just wants to hold onto the ball and run down the clock. Any scoring should only be by free throws.

This tactic should be used only in the last minute or so of the ball game. Too often, coaches begin their stall too quickly, taking their own players out of their momentum.

When running the *delay*, a team shouldn't even look to score. Its singular focus should be to keep the ball away from its opponents. To practice a stall, the plays shown in diagrams 11-1 and 11-2 should be run repeatedly. The ball should <u>change sides</u> often, and be kept out front. A team's players should never cross paths or they might be trapped by their defenders.

Zones

As many zones and zone variations exist as there are stars in the sky. It would take a volume so thick no one could print it for economic reasons to discuss each and every zone. The Five Player Open Post Motion Offense, however, offers several options that are very appropriate against all zones.

Diagrams 11-1 and 11-2 represent a basic offensive pattern against zones. The most profitable part of the change of sides would be the cut by the wing into the high post. The wing should be cutting to daylight while doing this maneuver. Should the wing get the ball, the movement by his teammates' Rules to Replace puts them in the holes of many zones. On the other hand, the wing can attack the basket with a dribble. The side-post curl cut can be incorporated into a team's zone attack (Diagram 1-5). This tactic creates another pass into the high-post region, an area where most zones are vulnerable.

Furthermore, cutting should not be overlooked against zones. Diagram 1-6 shows an excellent maneuver for the back-door lob near the basket. Diagrams 1-8, 1-9, 1-10, 1-11 show tactics that can be successful against zones.

Diagrams 3-7 and 3-8 also illustrate effective options for attacking zones. Diagram 4-9 shows a triangular overload attack that most coaches advocate using against zones. Diagram 5-1 offers a four-player overload that can be successfully used against zones.

Diagrams 5-2, 5-3, and 7-4 depict great maneuvers against zones. In addition, a team should not disregard using screens against zones, especially screens away and rolls back to the ball. Back screens can also be very effective against all types of zones.

Combinations

Combinations are as numerous as fish in the sea. To a point, it seems that all coaches have their own pet variation of the four-player zone and a chaser, or the three-zone defenders and two players chasing. The principles of attack in this instance involve at least three basic guidelines: set lots of screens for the player the defenders are chasing; get the ball inside to the team's big men; and set up the other outside shooters who can bomb the opponents into getting out of their combination zone and man defense.

All factors considered, a team wants to <u>change of sides</u> which will provide it with continuity (Diagrams 11-1 and 11-2). Diagrams 1-8, 1-9, 1-10, 1-11, 3-7, 3-8, 3-9, 3-10, 3-11, 5-1, 5-2, 5-3, and 7-4 also offer relevant assistance in this area.

A team should specialize its attack by knowing the offense extremely well and knowing its own personnel even better. For example, Diagrams 3-9, 3-10, and 5-1 could be highly effective against triangle-and-two defenses, whether inverted or played straight. On the other hand, a team might not want to use those plays in other situations, for example, against a box-and-one.

Traps

Defensive-minded coaches use all sorts of traps during the course of ball games. Some are employed during player-to-player defense, like trapping the first pass, or trapping in a specific area, or luring an offensive player into an area, then trapping. Others are more structured, like the 1-3-1 zone traps. It should not matter to a team which traps it is facing. A team should adhere to certain precepts as it attacks. For example, offensive players should never cross paths. When offensive players cross paths, the defenders are given the advantage. In fact, a team wants the offense spread even more if possible. This scenario makes the defenders run further to set their trap. It makes the interceptors have too great a territory to cover. Furthermore, it frequently causes the safety defender to have to cover two attackers near the basket.

When a team runs its change of sides, it wants its wing player, who is crossing the free-throw line, to come to meet a pass from the wing. At this point, the ball is in the most vulnerable position for the defenders. The wing has the dribble attack, and he should always look opposite for a quick pass to that area. The new receiver on the weakside has the choice to shoot or drive or pass inside to a cutting big man near the basket. Among the parts of the Five Players Open Post Offense that work extremely well against all sorts of traps are the following: Diagrams 11-1 and 11-2; Diagram 1-5, the side-post curl pattern; and Diagrams 1-8, 1-11, 5-1, 5-2, 5-3, and 7-4.

Several major tenets should be emphasized when considering traps, including: keep the offense spread; attack with a pass at or near high post; and look opposite, dump down to a cutter near the basket. Furthermore, a team should remember that since it has the skip pass in the basic offense, then a driving penetration before the defense can recover can be highly effective against a trapping team, especially if the offense has been spread a little further.

The Match-Up

To understand how to attack the match-up, a team should realize that the match-up is just like the person-to-person defense except that the defenders play an area. In person-to-person defense, the defenders on the strongside play person-to-person, while the defenders on the weakside offer help by playing a zone. In the match-up, the players play zone but use person-to-person techniques.

The area around the high post, especially the side-high post or medium post, is the most vulnerable to the match-up. Different-type cuts should be employed into this area. To get the ball to this area is one of the primary principles of play against a match-up zone. One of the two best ways to get the ball to the high post involves the wing cut in the change of sides (Diagrams 11-1 and 11-2). The wing, similar to that against regular zones, is cutting to daylight. The side-post curl, shown in Diagram 1-5, offers another effective entry into this exposed region, especially when it has been proceeded by a cutting wing, like in Diagram 1-6. Diagrams 1-8, 1-9, 1-10, 1-11, 3-7, 3-8, 5-1, 5-3, and 7-4 suggest other options against match-up defenses. A team facing a match-up wants lots of movement by both its personnel and the ball. This tactic compels the defenders to constantly change their coverage rules, thereby creating openings. A team wants to get the ball into the high-post region and make cuts when the ball is there.

Last-Second Shot

The Five Player Open Post Motion Offense allows a team to play for the last shot in each quarter, giving it four more possessions than its opponent, without it having to practice any differently. A team should consider following this basic principle: When the clock gets to thirty seconds (sometimes even forty-five seconds, if a team really wants to shorten the game (and it particularly wants to shorten the game when it is out manned), the ball should be held for the last shot. That last shot should be a good one—one that has been pre-practiced.

The question is how can a team best do this: The fundamental guideline is for a team to run the change of sides until the clock gets down to twelve seconds and then start its attack. This tactic gives it time to get a good shot and try for the offensive rebound if the situation dictates. It does not give itsopponents time to get a good shot even if they get the defensive rebound. This tactic should be practiced daily. The plays shown in Diagrams 11-1 and 11-2 should be run over and over and over until twelve seconds remain. A signal (a voice signal as well as visual one) should be used to let the players know to begin the scoring option. A team should not have to reset. Players are in their positions because of the Rules to Replace. Some of a team's best choices are illustrated in Diagrams 1-11, 2-2, 2-3, 2-4, 2-5, 2-6, 3-7, 3-8, 3-9, 3-10, 3-11, 5-3, 5-5, 6-3, and 7-4. Which options a team chooses to employ depends greatly on personal preference and the skills of its personnel at the time.

Summary

At this point in the text, a team has a complete offense, capable of attacking all known defenses. Coaches have the drills to teach it, to develop it, and to improve its execution. All that is left to address is knowing how to practice the offense team-wise to get the maximum effect for its strategy. That subject is covered in Chapter 13.

13

Team Drilling of the Offensive Strategies for the Five Player Open Post Offense

Just scrimmaging is not an appropriate way to effectively develop a fundamentally sound team. Scrimmaging should be conducted with a purpose. Focused scrimmaging not only enables a team to practice specific skills and techniques, it reinforces the learning of strategy. That's what this chapter is about.

5-On-0

5-on-0 is what coaches sometimes refer to as running the offense—dummy-style. Teams, however, don't want their players just running through their offense; they want their players practicing with a purpose. 5-on-0 practice involves five attackers and no defenders. A coach can stand on the sideline and yell specific instructions to his players that can be designed to keep them mentally alert to all the options of the offense.

A coach should make a list of at least 10 different types of patterns he wants his offense to run dummy-style daily. He can stand on the sideline and either call out those choices or can allow his players to make their cuts and call out what they are doing as they make those cuts.

A coach should have a specific idea concerning how many different maneuvers he wants his players to perform before attempting a shot. For example, change of sides into a back-door wing cut and exchange with the corner into another change of sides, followed by a corner screen and roll into a shot makes for a good series of options before the shot can be attempted. Once a coach really learns the offense, he can determine all kinds of choices for his players.

If a team is in pre-season workouts, it should run more options before it tries to score. That approach can be used to teach the players the offense more quickly. It is a relatively good idea for a team to run options that it plans to employ for its next opponent if the team is in mid- or late-season.

5-On-5, No Dribble

The "5-on-5, no-dribble" strategy eliminates part of a team's offense—a screen and roll, for example—because that technique requires a dribble. The "5-on-5, no-dribble" strategy, however, offers the advantage of compelling a team to include several other options in its offense, for example, change of sides, back-door and middle cuts, screens away from the ball, side-post curl, etc. It also impels a team's attackers to work together as a team to get the open shot. It is best to practice this scrimmage method when a team expects to see a zone defense (or a match-up) from its next opponent.

5-On-5, Designate A Scorer Or Two

The "5-on-5, designate a scorer or two" strategy is designed to bring a lot more screens into play. For example, a team designates "John" as the only person allowed to score during this possession. When the coach gets ready to designate "John", the offense should huddle away from the defense. The defense should not be allowed to know who has been designated as the team's scorer. Teammates will then try to free "John" by using a lot of screens.

This approach is an effective way to get more screening involved in a team's practicing. In addition, players become more aware of looking for the team's leading scorer — not just looking for the first open shot. It is best to use this tactic when a team is playing against an equal opponent the next game or when it is expecting to see a lot of combination defenses from its next opponent. This strategy is also very good practice for getting the last shot of each quarter.

5-On-5, Score Only On Lay-ups

The "5-on-5, score only on lay-ups" strategy provides a forum for really teaching team play. Again, a team's attackers should huddle away from the defenders in order to prevent the defense from knowing the attackers are using this strategy. Adhering to this strategy, players will always be looking toward the basket. Furthermore, they can use the entire offense to try to get this lay-up. This approach compels a team's players to really learn the Rules to Replace because they will constantly be forced to reset if they don't get the lay-up. This scrimmage strategy is best used when a team's players begin to employ too much one-on-one maneuvers during a ball game. This ploy has the desirable feature of bringing team play back into a team's offense.

5-On-5, Two Consecutive Stops

The "5-on-5, two consecutive stops" scrimmage strategy refers to the fact that if a team's attackers can score every other possession, they will be on offense all the time. The only way the defense gets to rotate to offense is to stop the offense two times in a row. This requirement includes offensive rebounding.

A team should not use this tactic if it will be facing a tough opponent in the next day or two. For example, a team's attackers (i.e., the first team) may have days when they are not at the top of their game, when their intensity and concentration levels are low. When that occurs, they will not be playing the best of offense. If a team is employing this scrimmaging strategy, a team's "first 5" might be on defense all practice. Understandably, they will not like this. A team should consider employing this tactic the day before a tough game, but only after its "first 5" has practiced scrimmaging offensively. The first team should be encouraged to realize the importance of getting that last shot each quarter.

5-On-5, Best Of Ten

On occasion, a coach should consider rewarding his team after practice in some tangible way (e.g., with food or sodas). An extra "stipend" could be given to the group of players who did the "best" in ten possessions. For example, the first team is given the ball ten times and attempts to score against the second team. The second team then has the ball for ten possessions. The first team should always be given the ball initially. That way, because they don't know how many times they will have to score to win the "best-of-ten competition", they will exert a maximum effort to score all of them.

Combinations

"Combinations" refers to the scrimmaging strategy that combines two of the aforementioned tactics. For example, a coach may call out "5-on-5, no dribble, score only on lay-ups". As a result, a team is practicing cuts, screens away from the ball, change of sides, Rules to Replace, and constant teamwork to get the lay-up. The point to remember is that a coach should carefully consider his choices when developing a scrimmaging strategy. The strategies that best prepare a team for its next opponent should be utilized. In other words, a coach should put some serious consideration into his practice plans before the team practices. The rewards can be immense.

Summary

Coaches have now been given the entire spectrum for introducing their offense, for teaching all the variations, for perfecting their team's offensive assault, and for scrimmaging its attack. Figuratively speaking, nothing has been left to chance. Success is within your team's grasp.

About the Author

Bob Huggins is the head men's basketball coach at West Virginia University, a position he assumed in 2007. Previously, he served in the same position at Kansas State University during the 2006 season. Before that, he was the head men's basketball coach at the University of Cincinnati from 1989 to 2005. During his 16 years at the helm of the Bearcats' program, Huggins compiled an impressive 399-127 record, making him the winningest coach in U.C. history. In the process, he led his last 14 Cincinnati squads to the NCAA Tournament—the third-longest streak among active coaches in the nation.

During his impressive career, Huggins has been awarded many coaching honors, including the Ray Meyer Award as the Conference USA Coach of the Year in 1997-98, 1998-99, and 1999-2000. He was named co-national coach of the year by *The Sporting News* in 2004-05 and was also *Basketball Times'* selection for national coach of the year for the 1997-98 season.

Huggins began his coaching career as a graduate assistant at his alma mater, the University of West Virginia, in 1977. Subsequent coaching stints included Ohio State (1978-80), Walsh College (1980-83), Central Florida (1983), and the University of Akron (1984-89). In his career, Huggins' teams have won 20 or more games in all but four of his 25 campaigns, including 30 or more twice.

Born in Morgantown, West Virginia, Huggins grew up in Gnadenhutten, Ohio, where he played high school basketball for his father, Charles Huggins, at Gnadenhutten Indian Valley South. Bob and his wife, June, have two daughters, Jenna and Jacqueline.